SOBERING DILEMMA

Sobering Dilemma
A History of Prohibition in British Columbia

DOUGLAS L. HAMILTON
Introduction by Jean Barman

Ronsdale Press

SOBERING DILEMMA
Copyright © 2004 Douglas L. Hamilton

All rights reserved. No part of this publication may be reproduced, stored in a retrieval system, or transmitted, in any form or by any means, without prior written permission of the publisher, or, in Canada, in the case of photocopying or other reprographic copying, a licence from Acess Copyright (Canadian Copyright Licensing Agency).

RONSDALE PRESS LTD.
3350 West 21st Avenue
Vancouver, B.C., Canada
V6S 1G7

Typesetting: Julie Cochrane, in New Baskerville 11 pt on 15
Cover Design: Julie Cochrane
Cover Photo: "Bootlegger with his car." Courtesy of BC Archives.
Paper: Ancient Forest Friendly Rolland "Enviro" — 100% post-consumer waste, totally chlorine-free and acid-free

Ronsdale Press wishes to thank the Canada Council for the Arts, the Government of Canada through the Book Publishing Industry Development Program (BPIDP), and the Province of British Columbia through the British Columbia Arts Council for their support of its publishing program.

Library and Archives Canada Cataloguing in Publication

Hamilton, Douglas L., 1945–
  Sobering dilemma: the history of prohibition in British Columbia / Douglas L. Hamilton; introduction by Jean Barman.

  Includes bibliographical references and index.
  ISBN 1-55380-016-8

  1. Prohibition — British Columbia — History. I. Title.
HV5091.C3H34 2004   363.4'1'09711   C2004-903310-7

At Ronsdale Press we are committed to protecting the environment. To this end we are working with Markets Initiative (www.oldgrowthfree.com) and printers to phase out our use of paper produced from ancient forests. This book is one step towards that goal.

Printed in Canada by AGMV Marquis

To the memory of my mother
Irene Till Hamilton

All laws which can be broken without injury
to another are counted but a laughing-stock, and
are so far from bridling the desires and lusts of
men, that on the contrary they stimulate them.
For "we are ever eager for forbidden fruit, and
desire what is denied." Nor do idle men ever lack
ability to elude the laws which are instituted about
things which cannot absolutely be forbidden.

— *Baruch de Spinoza, Of Aristocracy,* 1677

ACKNOWLEDGEMENTS

Every work of history is dependent on the labour of others. Anyone interested in government alcohol policy in British Columbia during the twentieth century owes a huge debt to Robert A. Campbell for his outstanding books and articles on the subject — in particular, *Demon Rum or Easy Money* and *Sit Down and Drink Your Beer*. Albert J. Hiebert's path-breaking MA thesis *Prohibition In British Columbia* (Simon Fraser University, 1969) was also immensely helpful.

Craig Heron's recent book, *Booze: A Distilled History,* provided a fascinating and useful perspective on liquor use in the rest of Canada. I would also like to thank the wonderful archivists at British Columbia Archives for providing me with a wealth of material that I did not realize even existed, especially the transcripts from the Commission to Investigate the Overseas Vote in 1917 and material from the BC Alcohol Research and Education Council. Permission to investigate the dusty files of the BC Provincial Police under the Freedom of Information and Protection of Privacy Act was also much appreciated.

I particularly wish to thank those whose many suggestions, corrections and encouragements did much to make this book possible: Robert A. Campbell, Wendy Wickwire, Shawn Cafferky, Ronald B. Hatch, Veronica Hatch, Jim Hogan, Penelope Clark, Fernanda Gonçalves, Gregory Evans, Erit Shimrat, Chris Bearchel, Annie Carrithers, Rick Waines, Peter Johnston and Sue Wheeler.

CONTENTS

Introduction by Jean Barman / 13

CHAPTER 1
ARDENT SPIRITS
God's Greatest Gift or the Devil's Servant? / 19

CHAPTER 2
BRITISH COLUMBIA'S FIRST LIQUOR PROHIBITION
Natives and Alcohol, 1854–1962 / 37

CHAPTER 3
REFORM, THE SOCIAL GOSPEL, AND
PREMIER RICHARD MCBRIDE / 62

CHAPTER 4
THE WAR, FOOD AND BOOZE / 80

CHAPTER 5
THE PURITY ELECTION OF 1916
"The Tighter the Law, the Fewer Get Tight" / 95

CHAPTER 6
DEMOCRACY OVERTURNED
The Soldiers' Vote, 1916–1917 / 110

CHAPTER 7
THE SECRET FILES OF THE
BRITISH COLUMBIA PROVINCIAL POLICE / 124

CHAPTER 8
CORRUPTION AND SCANDAL
Prohibition Discredited / 141

CHAPTER 9
THE TRIUMPH OF MODERATION / 162

CHAPTER 10
THE LIQUOR CONTROL BOARD AND
A NEW KIND OF BAR / 176

CONCLUSION / 194

Appendices / 199
Notes / 201
Bibliography / 211
Index / 219
About the Author / 224

INTRODUCTION
by Jean Barman

BEER, WINE, A MARTINI? What will you have?

But wait. Maybe it's not up to you or me to decide. Maybe it's not even possible to have a drink at all.

The decision whether or not to have a drink containing alcohol was in past time made by others on our behalf. It was not we who responded "yes" or "no," but rather self-designated moral arbiters acting in our supposed best interests. They were determined to control our access to beer, wine and spirits.

Historically, few commodities have agitated so many would-be reformers as has liquor. Convinced of their own superiority, men and women sought to prevent others from engaging in what was, from their perspective, improper behaviour. For some the goal was moderation or temperance; for others it was outright prohibition.

The movement for prohibition in British Columbia to some

extent reflected sentiment more generally across North America and beyond. The provincial campaigns for and against access to alcohol also had, as Douglas Hamilton convincingly demonstrates in *Sobering Dilemma,* distinctive features.

To understand the fervour liquor excited, we have to remind ourselves of the hold Christianity long exercised in Canada and across the Western world. In the nineteenth century adherents became convinced of their obligation to ensure not just their own salvation, but that of everyone else. Their determination to alter indigenous ways of life was one manifestation of this conviction, the movement for temperance and prohibition another.

It seemed inexplicable to erstwhile reformers that some men and women, particularly those whose way of life was unlike their own, would squander their hard-earned wages on drink. To this view was added an element of fear of bodies out of control by virtue of being intoxicated. Beer and wine, long part of everyday life, were bad enough; distilled spirits such as gin and rum were far worse in their effects. Something had to be done.

Protestants in particular turned their attention to creating "the kingdom of God" on earth as opposed to awaiting heaven. It was not just men who acted. Many women of the dominant society were looking for an acceptable means to gain some small measure of authority outside of the home, and the campaign against liquor consumption gave them the opportunity to do so. Reformers became convinced, in Hamilton's words, that if only liquor "could be eliminated, mankind, it was prophesied by the true believers, would return to a state that would resemble the garden paradise of Adam and Eve." Canada would become a kind of heaven on earth.

It seemed for a time as if the reformers would triumph. Prohibition was enacted in Prince Edward Island in 1901, and some other provinces restricted public drinking. Quebec was the principal holdout, not surprising given its Roman Catholic ethos. The First World War gave prohibitionists the boost they needed. Successfully portraying drinking as unpatriotic, they closed down the alcohol business across the country. "Canada was engaged in a duel to the death, and the use of liquor struck at the very heart of the war effort. It not only stole precious food; it also distracted and befuddled soldiers and workers." Following a provincial vote, prohibition took effect in British Columbia on October 1, 1917.

Douglas Hamilton's choice of title, *Sobering Dilemma,* captures the weakness of the prohibitionist movement. It offered what he quite rightly terms "simple solutions" to complex issues. Aboriginal people would not be made amenable by denying them the right to drink. Nor would the problems of social dislocation caused by industrialization, urbanization and then the First World War be solved by closing down working people's principal places of relaxation — bars, taverns and saloons. Many soldiers were opposed: the opportunity for a drink was one of the few diversions from hard-fought battles.

Douglas pays particularly close attention to the Prohibition Act of 1916, subsequent provincial votes for and against prohibition, and the secret files of the BC Provincial Police. He argues persuasively that the prohibition legislation was not just race-based in forbidding drink to Aboriginal people but also class- and place-based in its loopholes for the well-off, particularly if living in a big city. It "helped to be white" and to reside in Vancouver or Victoria rather than in interior towns where "even minor violators were shown little mercy." In addition, "wealthy tipplers could import from out of province" or "obtain legal booze through a doctor's prescription."

In just three years British Columbians decisively changed their view on prohibition, being the first province after Quebec to do so. In a plebiscite held on October 20, 1920, only 55,000 British Columbians voted to stick with prohibition compared to 92,000 voting for a system of government control of liquor which continues to the present day. Only two municipalities in the entire province — Richmond and Chilliwack — favoured the status quo. The first British Columbia government liquor store opened the next June 15th, the same day that prohibition was repealed. Public drinking establishments were not permitted until 1925 and then in far more restricted forms than had earlier been the case.

Other provinces gradually followed suit. The longest to hold out were, not unexpectedly, the firmly Protestant provinces of Nova Scotia to 1930 and Prince Edward Island to 1948. Public drinking was banned in the Maritimes until after the Second World War, in New Brunswick and Prince Edward Island to the 1960s. Only in that decade were Aboriginal people treated like other Canadians in respect to access to liquor.

Sobering Dilemma's dissection of the movements for and against prohibition in British Columbia goes beyond the usual explanations. The province was drawn into the reform rhetoric through the particular circumstances of war, but British Columbians never gave the movement the wide-ranging support received elsewhere in English Canada.

A number of factors made British Columbia distinctive. Hamilton points out that "no other province in Canada contained such a high proportion of immigrants from the British Isles," most of whom "regarded the anti-liquor fanaticism of the Methodists and others with scepticism, even disdain." In 1921 six out of every ten immigrant British Columbians were born in Britain. The province also contained a large number of seasonal workers who, during their off months, needed some means for passing the time. Women's attraction to the cause was not as whole hearted as it might have been. They supported prohibition as a complement to suffrage, but only until they won the right to vote. Returned veterans were in general opposed. Some British Columbians fretted that prohibition was having a negative effect by increasing the use of other drugs.

Hamilton turns our attention to civil rights and to economic self-interest. Enforcement was extraordinarily difficult. "If prohibition meant posting a guard in every household, the price in liberty and privacy would be too much to bear." He dissects what he terms "the liquor patronage machine," which was closely aligned to provincial officials. There was big money to be made in alcohol, not just for friends of those in government but, increasingly, through licensing and taxation. Government liquor stores continue to bring large amounts of revenue into provincial coffers.

Today British Columbians take access to beer, wine and spirits for granted. We don't have a second thought in responding to the question of whether or not we want a drink containing alcohol. Perhaps we should. We may have come to a consensus on prohibition, but the fight has many echoes that reverberate into the present day.

The object of our zeal varies over time, but the underlying dynamic does not much alter. It is still often the case that the expense of enforcement, together with the economic benefits lost to government, is very able, as with prohibition, to render regulations inert. *Sobering Dilemma* offers an object lesson in how reform, whatever the target, is sometimes easier to enact than to sustain. We need to think through the feasibility of our desires.

Moral certainty, racism, fear of drunkenness — they all played a role in demonizing liquor. We are still prone to act as moral arbiters, and our reasons may be just as temporal as were those of prohibitionists. Be it marijuana possession, prostitution, big box stores, or any one of a number of current issues, we take stands in others' supposed best interests. Perhaps we are correct in doing so, but at the least we should examine our motives. *Sobering Dilemma* reminds us of the dangers of smugness in thinking that we have the answers on behalf of others.

— Jean Barman
August 2004

CHAPTER 1

ARDENT SPIRITS
God's Greatest Gift or the Devil's Servant?

WOULDN'T IT BE WONDERFUL if we could cure the worst problems facing society by making one small change in human behaviour? If we could just refrain from one fatal vice, then poverty, immorality, ill health, crime, insanity, accidents, sloth, incompetence, ill will, prostitution and drunkenness would all vanish from the earth. Many would find this view absurdly simplistic today, but it was once the accepted conventional wisdom in much of North America. The idea that spirituous liquors are at the root of most of the evils in society is not new; the nineteenth and early twentieth centuries saw the culmination of the greatest crusade the world has ever witnessed against an intoxicating drug. Alcohol had come to be blamed for just about everything. If only it could be eliminated, mankind, it was prophesied by the true believers, would return to a state that would resemble the garden paradise of Adam and Eve.

Traditional explanations for mankind's love of intoxicating stimulants run the gamut from moral weakness to mental illness. During the nineteenth and early twentieth centuries, most identified individual moral failings as the root cause, and this legitimized the harsh treatment of offenders. The outright prohibition of selected intoxicants remains today the preferred method of dealing with these substances. Yet science suggests that intoxication and addiction have an appeal that goes far beyond moral turpitude. Animals as well as humans will do almost anything to alter their consciousness. The literature is full of thousands of examples, including unsteady cows grazing on locoweed, inebriated cats unable to stay away from catnip, birds growing tipsy on fermenting fruit, bumblebees passing out among the flowers, and African elephants breaking into village brewing vats and going on a drunken rampage. Ronald Siegel, in *Intoxication: Life in Pursuit of Artificial Paradise*, argues that throughout our entire history as a species, intoxication has been a basic drive similar to hunger, thirst, or sex, and sometimes overshadowing all other activities in life:

> Recent ethological and laboratory studies with colonies of rodents and islands of primates, and analysis of social and biological history, suggest that the pursuit of intoxication with drugs is a primary motivational force in the behaviour of organisms. Our nervous system, like those of rodents and primates, is arranged to respond to chemical intoxicants in much the same way it responds to rewards of food, drink, and sex.[1]

And just because someone abstains from drugs does not mean they are saying no to intoxication. Modern research shows that many activities can bring on a euphoric mental state. Running, competitive sports, music and meditation are good examples. Although none of these drugs or activities is essential for life, as are food and drink, many individuals will pursue them as if they were. This desire to escape to a new place and embrace a different mental state seems to be part of the web of life for both animals and humans. If this is true, the sledgehammers of police and prison are exceedingly crude tools when it comes to suppressing what may well be a basic desire. For better or worse, people feel driven to alter their consciousness, and attempts to legislate on such matters create a dilemma worse than the one the lawmakers were trying to solve in the first place.

The movement for the abolition of alcohol did not appear overnight. In order to understand how it developed into one of the first great mass movements in modern North American history, we should first take a brief look at the changes in alcohol use that resulted from the introduction of distilled spirits, and the early temperance response to the crisis these changes created.

In the beginning, there was booze. Long before humans trod the planet, fruits ripened, rotted and fermented, producing ethyl alcohol. Insects, birds and mammals were powerfully attracted to this strange refreshment and were quick to partake. Of all the intoxicants used in the world today, alcohol has been around the longest. Human fondness for drink predates the use of cannabis, opium, coca, tea and coffee. The Sumerians quaffed their beer, the Celts guzzled mead, and the Greeks and Romans downed grape wine in prodigious quantities. People certainly overindulged, but alcoholism was not seen as a major social problem before the eighteenth century. This was because the alcoholic content of the beer, mead and wine of those times amounted to only 5 to 10 percent, so the considerable quantity required for inebriation worked against overindulgence. The widespread distribution of distilled spirits in relatively recent times, however, has marked a decisive change in the way alcohol is used and perceived worldwide.

Distillation of fermented beverages goes back thousands of years. The idea of separating a liquid into its various components, which differ in their boiling points, was probably rediscovered many times in the ancient world. Credible sources describe the existence of distilled spirits in China about 3000 B.C., India in 2500 B.C. and Egypt in 2000 B.C. The most common process employed vats of boiling wine covered with sheep's wool or other absorbent material. The alcohol evaporated and condensed on the wool, where it could be squeezed out and collected. This method proved inefficient and expensive, and the distilled liquor was used mainly in perfumes and exotic medicines.

Arab alchemists practised distillation in medieval times, keeping their methods a professional secret. The world "alcohol" itself comes from the Arabic, and Arab alchemists refined and simplified the process around 800 A.D. For many centuries this exotic liquid remained a mere curiosity — a peculiar fluid that would cool the skin yet was also highly flammable. Then, in the thirteenth century, a Frenchman — Arnauld de Villeneuve — invented a method of distilling wine into a potion he dubbed *aqua vitae,* or "water of life." A flask of glass, copper, tin or ceramic was filled with wine and capped with a tightly fitting cover with a long beak. The flask, cap and beak together came to be called the alembic. When heated, the hot concentrated alcohol rose and condensed in the beak where it could be directed into a receptacle. Four or five drops of this miraculous fluid taken daily were guaranteed to prolong and enhance life. In fact, as Raphael Holinshed notes in his *Chronicles of England, Scotland and Ireland* (published in 1577), *aqua vitae* cured just about everything:

> It sloweth age; strengtheneth youth; it helpeth digestion; it cutteth flegm; it abandoneth melancholia; it relisheth the heart; it highlighteth the mind; it quickeneth the spirits; it cureth the hydropsie; it expelleth the gravel; it puffeth away ventosity; it keepeth and preserveth the head from whirling, the eyes from dazzling; the tongue from lisping, the teeth from chattering, the hands from shivering, the sinews from shrinking, the veins from crumbling, the bones from aching, the marrow from soaking. . . .[2]

In other words, *aqua vitae* was the miracle restorative, with properties similar to the "philosopher's stone." There was considerable interest in this new "medicine," and a number of books on distillation became bestsellers in Europe, going through numerous printings and translations during the sixteenth century. The best known of these do-it-yourself classics was the 1501 *Liber de arte Distillandi*

(Book of the Distilling Art) by Hieronymus Brunschwygk. The interest sparked several important technical improvements in the design of stills around this time. In 1526, the alchemist Paracelsus introduced the use of a cooling water bath for the alembic, which stabilized the brew's temperature and prevented the flask from cracking. The vapour cooling was also greatly improved by running the condensing tube through cold water. Within a few decades, distilled spirits were no longer a novelty.

The great wars that swept through Europe in the sixteenth and seventeenth centuries created social turmoil, millions of desperate refugees and a great fondness for this new beverage. Many found that *aqua vitae* not only cured their ills, but also provided solace, warmth and escape from tribulation. These years did much to ensure the acceptance of what came to be called "ardent spirits" in the daily life of millions, and many countries were soon producing their own variants. Poland had its vodka, Holland its gin, Mexico its tequila, Ireland its whiskey, the West Indies their rum, and France and Italy their brandy. By 1694, England was churning out 4 million gallons of gin a year. This figure rose to 11 million gallons by 1733 as the price fell. Very quickly, a host of social problems became associated with the use of distilled spirits.

The great English painter William Hogarth may have put it best, in his famous set of 1751 engravings contrasting *Gin Lane* and *Beer Street*. In *Gin Lane,* a grinning drunken woman with breasts exposed reaches for a pinch of snuff, and drops her child headfirst over a steep railing. A ragged carpenter pawns his tools, and a housewife her pots and pans, to buy gin. A suicide can be seen hanging limply in the upper right-hand corner of a disintegrating house. The sign over the entrance of a gin cellar reads, "Drunk for a Penny/Dead Drunk for Two Pence/Clean Straw for Nothing." By contrast, his engraving *Beer Street* shows prosperous patrons swilling beer with friends. The caption reads "All is joyous and thriving. Industry and jollity go hand in hand." Everyone is healthy and well-dressed; only the pawnshop seems in disrepair.

The British Parliament found the abuse of spirits so threatening that it passed a number of Acts to control it. The petition accompanying the Gin Act of 1736 claimed that "thousands of His Majesty's subjects" had perished because of alcohol, and many others were "unfit for useful labor, debauched in morals and drawn into all kinds of wickedness."[3] Henry Fielding, novelist and social reformer, commented in a 1751 pamphlet, "Should the drinking of this poison be continued at its present height, during the next twenty years, there will be by that time very few of the common people left to drink it."[4]

The sudden availability of distilled alcohol presented a new and dangerous threat to society that was unlike anything seen before. Highly concentrated alcohol amounted to a completely new drug, one that affected people entirely differently from lighter beer and wines. It was far more addictive, deadly poisonous when consumed in quantity, and its introduction precipitated a public health disaster on a scale not seen since the Black Death. This sudden availability radically changed age-old drinking habits. Now, instead of spending a long evening getting tipsy with friends, one quickly ended up besotted and insensible on the floor. Much like today's crack cocaine and heroin, which also concentrate relatively weak plant intoxicants, these "ardent spirits" turned a relatively harmless pastime into something far more dangerous. Early prohibition movements in Germany, England, Ireland, Australia, New Zealand, Finland, Iceland, Norway, the Netherlands, Switzerland and, later, Russia, France and Italy were focused entirely on spirits. Cider, beer and wine were considered acceptable, and even healthy.

North America did not long escape the ravages of distilled spirits. Rum and whiskey (which was often referred to as brandy) had been introduced early into the fur trade, and also became part of the great triangle of the slave trade in the Atlantic. Africans were traded in the Caribbean for molasses, which was shipped to New England and converted into rum, which was then taken back to Africa to exchange for more slaves. Sweetness in all its varieties gives "life" to fermentation, and sugar was scarce and expensive in Europe before the eighteenth century. After sugar cane was introduced into the Caribbean West Indies around 1650, it rapidly became the world's most valuable trading commodity. The plant, originally from Asia, thrived in its new environment and production skyrocketed. It is estimated that between 1713 and 1792, Great Britain alone imported about £162,000,000 worth of goods — almost all of it sugar. Much of this new mountain of sugar was used in the production of gin, causing the price of the latter to fall drastically. The small sugar-producing islands of Jamaica, Barbados and St. Kitts dominated the New World economy, while the vast mainland nearby was considered a hopeless liability. After the humiliating loss of her extensive colonies in North America after 1763, France felt little pain as she retained ownership of the far more profitable sugar islands of Martinique and Guadeloupe.

Dr. Benjamin Rush, America's first Surgeon General, was one of the first on this side of the Atlantic to call into question the widely held view that alcohol was beneficial to human health. A Quaker, and the most prominent physician of his age, Rush was also a charter member of America's anti-slavery movement. In 1785, Rush published the enormously influential *An Inquiry into the Effects of Ardent Spirits on the Human Body and Mind*. For the first time, the dangers of hard liquor were clearly laid out by a physician in authority, while its mythical health benefits were debunked. Rush observed that liquor had no food value and was habit-forming, and that continual use caused memory loss, physical deterioration and moral decay. Furthermore, use of distilled alcohol led to immodest and extravagant actions such as "singing, hallooing, roaring, imitating the noises of brute animals, jumping, tearing off clothes, dancing naked, breaking glasses and china." Rather than curing diseases, hard drink caused them. Among the most acute were the following:

1. Decay of appetite, sickness at stomach, puking of bile and discharging of frothy and viscous phlegm.
2. Obstruction of the liver.
3. Jaundice and dropping of belly and limbs, and finally every cavity of the body.

4. Hoarseness and a husky cough, leading to consumption.
5. Diabetes, i.e. a frequent and weakening discharge of pale or sweetish urine.
6. Redness and eruptions in different parts of the body, rumbuds, a form of leprosy.
7. A fetid breath.
8. Frequent and disgusting belchings.
9. Epilepsy.
10. Gout.
11. Madness — one third of patients confined owed their conditions to ardent spirits.[5]

Rush observed as well that most of the diseases caused by distilled liquor were of "a mortal nature." Significantly, Rush did not regard beer or wine as dangerous, and even encouraged moderate use of wine to preserve health and longevity. He felt that the obvious dangers of distilled alcohol would ensure that their use would remain a temporary aberration, soon to be replaced by the consumption of weaker stimulants. Even opium was to be preferred over rum and whiskey.

To mitigate the evils of alcohol, Rush proposed a number of remedies. He called on government authorities to limit the number of taverns, levy higher taxes on liquor and confiscate the property of habitual drinkers. Drunkards should be incarcerated, and their possessions turned over to a court-appointed trustee for the benefit of their families. Churches should forbid the use of "ardent spirits" under canonical law, as the Quakers had done, and declare them to be contraband. The Surgeon General's path-breaking book laid the groundwork for prohibition in North America, and its observations and remedies became an integral part of the ideology of the movement. But Rush stressed temperance over prohibition, and his refusal to condemn all alcoholic beverages would end up sowing division and confusion in the years ahead.

The argument between the supporters of temperance and the advocates of complete abstinence was never satisfactorily resolved. Were the physical and social disasters associated with drink caused by the abuse of a very good thing, or the use of a very bad thing? Part of the problem stemmed from the way people viewed the nature of intoxication. Many North Americans did not really believe that beer, cider and wine were, in fact, intoxicating. Yes, people could get drunk on these beverages, but it took a great deal of effort. Normal use did not cause intoxication. Eliminate distilled liquor, instead, and society's problems with drink would be solved. Nevertheless, during the 1840s the abstinence groups gained the upper hand, and their popularity increased. Some began to demand a new pledge of total abstinence from members, who would mark a "T" after their name for *total* abstinence, hence the term "teetotaler." Those who broke their promise were expelled in disgrace.

The temperance movement gained an early foothold in British Columbia. With the discovery of gold on the Fraser River, the viability of the colonies of Vancouver Island and British Columbia was assured. Upward of 25,000 miners, mostly Americans, suddenly disembarked to make their fortunes, and completely overwhelmed the few hundred white settlers who occupied Victoria and a few other trading posts. Gold mining was hard seasonal work in mid-nineteenth-century British Columbia. Miners panned and sluiced in the summer and part of the spring and fall, when water levels were low. After the rains began, they returned to Victoria with a poke of gold and much free time. This was a sure recipe for trouble. In 1862, the Anglican Bishop of Oxford, Samuel Wilberforce, spoke in London about the situation in the twin colonies of Vancouver Island and British Columbia. Gold miners, he said,

> . . . have but a short harvest of a few weeks in the gold fields, and then, all unused to the possession of wealth, all unfitted for its spending, all unable to invest it with no calls of the family upon them, no natural and healthy outlets for their new infusion of this new gold, go down for the rest of the year to some city upon the border of that land, and find there the leeches of dissipation and corruption, of lust, and of drunkenness, ready to relieve them of the plethora of that unusual fullness, and so are exposed to a new

form and set of temptations, against which nothing but habits of morality and religion deeply ingrained into their own nature will defend poor weak human beings suddenly subjected to them.[6]

For the settlers of the few towns in the twin colonies, the streets seemed full of drunken rowdies, shady gamblers, thieving camp followers and prostitutes of every colour. Many of the more permanent settlers soon came to deplore the noise, turmoil and lack of security, and called for amelioration. A British Columbia Constabulary (later called the British Columbia Provincial Police) was organized in 1858 to bring order to the gold fields, and word went out calling for the calming guidance of Protestant Christianity.

Among the first ministers to arrive were a group of four Wesleyan Methodist missionaries from Ontario in 1859. They established congregations in Victoria, New Westminster, Nanaimo and Hope, preaching the need for personal conversion, strict observation of the Sabbath, and the complete elimination of alcohol. A Congregationalist mission followed, along with a Presbyterian group from Ulster in 1862. There were soon moves to import the temperance organizations that were proving so effective in the rest of North America.

The ministers turned to the Sons of Temperance, founded in New York's Teetotaler's Hall in 1842, and branches of the Sons were established in Victoria and Hope in 1859. Like many nineteenth-century civic organizations, the Sons was preoccupied with regalia, uniforms and elaborate ceremonies. Members greeted each other as "Great worthy brother," wore lily-white robes, and displayed a six-pointed star within a triangle as their standard. Women joined the Daughters of Temperance, and even the children were not left out. They had their own Cadets of Temperance, which were provided with appropriate study materials. These groups proved highly popular, numbering 6,000 divisions with 250,000 members in America by 1860.[7]

Numerous offshoots and variants appeared all over the continent, such as the Templars of Honor and Temperance, the Knights of Jericho, the Daughters of Samaria, the Temperance Flying

Artillery and the Independent Order of Good Templars. This last was accused of being a "free love society," because it was one of the first civic organizations to accept both men and women as members.

Those who found the bizarre paraphernalia and rituals of the Sons of Temperance strange could always join a more moderate group like the Dashaway Clubs. The Dashaways were formed in San Francisco in 1859 when four young blades on a drunken bender unaccountably decided to desist and "dash away the flowing bowl." Instead of demanding a pledge of permanent abstinence, they signed members on for a six- to twelve-month period (medical purposes excepted with a doctor's letter). In place of the saloon and dancehall, they provided places for meetings, a library for quiet reading, and a gym for workouts. Amor de Cosmos, a leading member of the Victoria community, became a charter member and their west coast printer. Wisely, they avoided divisive discussions of religion or politics; the mere mention of "sectarian or party politics" brought a reprimand for a first offence and a five dollar fine for further infractions.[8] These clubs were very popular and raised public awareness of the problems of alcohol, but they were primarily civic organizations without political influence.

In spite of the plethora of temperance organizations, the mass movement for temperance was having only moderate success in the rest of British North America. By 1852, half a million people had taken the pledge — about one-quarter to one-third of the total population, but this obviously did not constitute a majority. There seemed little to show for all of the preaching, petitioning and pledging. Moral example and education had been the main tools of persuasion, but they were proving ineffective. Many were becoming impatient with empty talk, and argued that moral persuasion and self-discipline alone were not going to stem the evils of drink. Some new and powerful weapon was needed that could put the liquor interests out of business once and for all. Prohibition would be imposed from above, using the formidable powers of the State to act as enforcer. The inspiration for this brilliant new strategy came from a man named Neal Dow.

Born in Maine in 1804, Dow came to be known worldwide as the "Napoleon of Temperance" for his relentless struggle against demon alcohol. He was quick with his fists, prone to explosive rages, and a believer in activist "muscular Christianity." Upright men, he felt, should set the example to protect public morality, for drunkenness was at the root of all poverty, depravity and family disintegration. Dow was a successful merchant, politically ambitious and, like Rush, a devoted anti-slavery abolitionist. But instead of relying on moral persuasion and self-discipline, Dow turned to the police, courts and jails as his allies in rooting out the drinking scourge. He pushed hard for strict state laws banning the manufacture and sale of all alcohol. Using words like "crusade," "battle," "war" and "victory," he breathed new life into the struggle.

Dow's efforts were crowned by success in 1851 when he was elected mayor of Portland, Maine, and his Act for the Suppression of Drinking Houses was passed by the state legislature. The idea immediately caught on, and, within four years, thirteen states passed similar legislation, although some still permitted the use of beer and wine. These remarkable victories led to speaking tours before huge crowds in Australia, Britain and the Maritime colonies, which helped make Dow's name a household word. New Brunswick passed its own Maine-style law in 1856, but riots broke out and the Act proved unenforceable. The British government apparently had doubts about the controversial legislation, and called for new elections in New Brunswick. When the new regime scrapped the Act, many were convinced that Dow's experiment would never work in Canada.

There were increasing doubts that it could work even in Maine. Dow's statutes were proving impossible to enforce. While the sale of liquor could be made illegal, there was no law against giving alcohol away. It became a common practice to vend a pickle or a cracker to patrons, which came with a free drink. Soon saloon flunkies became even more creative, selling tickets for the viewing of fictitious attractions such as a blind pig — which happened to include a free shot or two. Thus the term "blind pig" came to mean an illegal drinking establishment in the same way that "speakeasy" would be used in the 1930s. Within a few years, all states but Maine had abandoned the new liquor laws.

Neal Dow became increasingly fanatical as he watched his great achievement founder. In Portland he led raids on saloons, hired spies and informants, encouraged vigilante groups, set up special police courts to guarantee a guilty verdict, and instructed police to search all trains, wagons and ships in the city for contraband. Yet drink was still easy to find in the city — and anywhere else in Maine, for that matter. Although Dow's fascination with using laws, courts and punishment as a way of stopping drinking seemed to be destined to failure at this period, his tactics marked a significant escalation in the war against alcohol.

The trauma of the American Civil War ended interest in prohibition for the next decade in the United States, but the movement slowly gained strength north of the border. The drinking of alcohol was banned from many workplaces, including the Hudson's Bay Company, coal mines, factories and rural work camps. But this pattern did not hold for British Columbia. More alcohol per capita was consumed in the province than anywhere else in Canada, and much of this was hard liquor. When the 1896 Royal Commission on the Liquor Traffic published its findings, British Columbians were not surprised to find themselves way ahead of the rest of Canada in every category of drink.

YEARLY PER CAPITA CONSUMPTION OF
ALCOHOL IN GALLONS (1893)

Dominion average	.597
Ontario	.654
Quebec	.672
Nova Scotia	.305
New Brunswick	.362
Manitoba	.153
British Columbia	1.262

To understand this high consumption of alcohol in British Columbia even as the temperance movement was growing in strength, one has to realize that, in ways we can barely comprehend today, alcohol played a central role in the life of many people across North America. The day would start with a healthy dollop of whiskey for every member of the family, often including children. This was followed by an 11 a.m. grog break. Wine and beer accompanied a hearty lunch, with further refreshment for a 4 p.m. break. Port and wine were served with supper, and then the family retired to a nearby tavern to hear the latest news and gossip. Spirits, in particular, were used to celebrate births, weddings, christenings, wakes and holidays. They were also used on the job to urge on the workers and to celebrate important accomplishments. No business contract was properly concluded without a toast, and liquor glorified the reign of God, king and country. Stores often placed cups and a pail of whiskey at the door so shoppers could relax and refresh themselves for free. No picnic or sports day was considered complete without a liquor stand (usually run by the local hotel) to supply refreshment after a game of "climbing the greasy pole" or "walking the bowsprit."[10]

The poorer classes and the Natives preferred cheap imported rum and whiskey; the rich went for sweet wines, like port, and the fiery arak made in the Middle East from palms. Most distilled liquor arrived from Ontario, the United States and Great Britain where quality was high and prices low. Being concentrated and valuable, it was a favourite cargo on incoming ships. Home-made hooch was also widely available along with the highly popular locally produced beer. After William Steinberger established British Columbia's first brewery near Victoria in 1858, many others followed his example. By 1880 there were nine legal breweries; in 1890, there were eighteen; and by 1900, forty-one legal breweries throughout the province.[11] A rudimentary transportation infrastructure combined with a lack of refrigeration forced beer makers to produce small batches for nearby markets. Small breweries could be found in almost every town with a population of more than a thousand, often as part of a hotel or tavern business. As brewing techniques improved along with transportation, a great wave of consolidation took place in the brewing industry in the early twentieth century. The decline of small company towns in the province together with increasing urbanization favoured the larger urban producers such as the Victoria-Phoenix Company in Esquimalt and the Silver Spring Brewery in Victoria. The number of breweries in British Columbia fell to thirty-one by 1910; and to only thirteen in 1920, the last year of prohibition.[12]

For thirsty tipplers of the nineteenth century, the cheapest and easiest place to find a drink was the local saloon, but it was far more than a place to drink. These establishments were the social center for most communities. Men went to the saloon to drink, eat, sleep, exchange gossip, gamble, pick up the mail, find a job, cash a cheque, play cards, hear the news and sometimes even attend church. Usually open twenty-four hours a day, seven days a week (until the turn of the century), the saloon was a place of recreation where one could take in a boxing match, magic show or cock fight, watch a play or variety acts and pursue the few available women. As early as the 1860s, lonely men could buy a dance from a hurdy-gurdy girl for a dollar. The *Cariboo Sentinel* noted:

> The hurdy style of dancing differs from all other schools. If you ever saw a ring of bells in motion, you have seen the exact positions these young ladies are put through during the dance, the more muscular the partner, the nearer the approximation of the ladies' pedal extremities to the ceiling, and the gent who can hoist his "gal" the highest is the best dancer.[13]

Weddings, christenings, dances and union meetings were held in saloons. Drinking establishments were small, friendly and plentiful, and often provided the only public toilets in town. John Pawson, who once owned a saloon in Nanaimo, described the bar scene of early British Columbia in the late 1800s:

> In the early days the saloon was like the club. There were at that time none of the home comforts that are found in the older settled

communities, and in fact there were very few of the home comforts that exist at the present time. At that time men lived in cabins and lived roughly. Many of them lived with Indian women, and the consequence was that in the saloon you would hear the latest gossip, for news came but once a week, and there were no telegraphs. So the saloon was a rendezvous for the men to a greater extent than it is now.[14]

Pawson noted also that the many different activities in the early saloons attracted a different crowd, or what he termed "a different class of people." In other words, where the later saloons were principally places to drink, the earlier saloons were social centers.

The saloons were also the cheapest place in town to eat. The attractive trays of free food served a dual purpose: they drew in hungry patrons from the streets and whetted their thirst with a massive dose of salt. Peanuts, pickles, pretzels, sauerkraut, pickled herring and sausage were favourites. There were no age limits and it was not uncommon in the afternoon for a bar to fill with thirsty teenagers on their way home from school.

Emily Carr, in *The Book of Small*, describes an adventure she had as a child in the 1880s, when a herd of wild cattle on their way to market came stampeding down Fort Street in Victoria. A friendly patron pulled Carr into safety in the Bee Hive Saloon:

> I looked around the Saloon. Shiny taps were beside me and behind the long counter-bar ran shelves full of bottles and sparkling glasses; behind them again was a looking-glass so that there seemed to be twice as many bottles as there really were, and two barmen and two negroes and two me's! In the back half of the saloon were barrels and small wooden tables; chairs with round backs stood about the floor with their legs sunk in sawdust; bright brass spittoons were everywhere. The saloon was full of the smell of beer and of sawdust.[15]

While the young Emily saw the saloon as something magical and a place of safety, many others in the community perceived it as having a much darker side. To hide any evils lurking within, saloon doors were usually shuttered, and the windows blocked with advertising, potted plants or bottles. And certainly they were not always the most salubrious of establishments. A thick layer of sawdust covered the floor to soak up spilled drinks and tobacco juice that missed the spittoon. Posters of voluptuous nudes competed with circulars advertising bare-knuckle prizefighters like George Wilson the "Cariboo Champion" and George Baker the "Canadian Pet." Binge drinking was the norm. People drank to get loaded, usually as quickly as possible. Payday arrived and the workforce would head en masse for the bar. Assaults and drunkenness were the main law enforcement issues facing police in turn-of-the-century British Columbia. Drunkenness contributed to accidents, lost work time, crime, broken homes, poverty, gambling, prostitution and a host of other social problems.

The important role of the saloons can be seen in the way that they always seemed to be the very first buildings to go up in a new town. By 1900 there were more than a thousand places to buy a drink in British Columbia, from the fancy to the downright squalid. By 1880, there was one licensed bar for every thirteen people in New Westminster, and more than 100 liquor licences issued for Victoria. In early Vancouver, saloons outnumbered other stores, and the competition forced bar owners to push their product aggressively. The coal mining town of Nanaimo had twenty-one legal outlets and many more illicit ones serving a population of some six thousand residents. An elderly miner remembered the booming liquor business in Ladysmith when he was a teenager:

> There were fifteen hotels and everyone of 'em was doin' business. And there was also a brewery and another place up on the hill that was a wholesale liquor place. Beer was $1.50 for a dozen big quarts. I worked at Simon Leiser's General Store and he sold a bottle of Scotch for $1.25. Beer was all five cents a glass. One of the men I worked with sent me for a bottle of whiskey for him every working day of the week. Of course, it suited me to go. I'd sneak a smoke and then rap on the door of the old Frank Hotel and they'd bring me out a shandy while I was waitin' for the whiskey.[16]

There were so many hotels and saloons that the sale of liquor without a licence became routine, with drinks being cheap and outlets competing openly, offering enticing incentives such as free entertainment or drinks to draw in customers.

One needed no directions to find the local bar. The smell of spilled beer and tobacco smoke wafted out into the street along with boisterous voices. Refuse and filth littered the area, while drunken derelicts pawed at passersby. A gaggle of children would cluster around the unsteady, teasing them in the streets — and robbing them in the alleyways. Fights were frequent, and hotel visitors complained of noise, which usually did not let up until the festivities ended at 8 a.m. with a final "God Save the Queen." For better or worse, it is clear that alcohol played an important role in almost everyone's life in late nineteenth-century British Columbia. The temperance movement faced a number of imposing obstacles, and it was going to have a difficult time selling its message to the province before it could succeed in 1917.

CHAPTER 2

BRITISH COLUMBIA'S FIRST LIQUOR PROHIBITION
Natives and Alcohol, 1854–1962

"IT IS UNLAWFUL FOR any person to give, sell or barter intoxicating liquor to an Indian, or to permit or suffer the same to be given, sold, or bartered, as aforesaid, to be consumed by any Indian in such person's abode, shop, store, bar-room, boat, canoe, or other premises; and every person so doing shall on conviction before any justice of the peace, forfeit and pay a fine of not more than one hundred pounds sterling for the first offense, together with the costs of conviction. . . . In the event of a second conviction for any offence under this Act or in the case of a first conviction, if default shall be made in payment of any fine imposed by the Act, the convicting magistrate is empowered to commit the person or persons so convicted to the common jail, with or without hard labor, for a term of not less than one, or more than twelve, calendar months; and the magistrate may award one moiety of the fines recovered to or among any informers."[1]

Prohibition for British Columbia's First Nations people is a huge and complex topic that deserves a book of its own. Nonetheless, an abbreviated chapter is included for two reasons. First, because it is a little-known but important part of British Columbia's history. And second, because it demonstrates how laws against substance abuse can be used against selected targets for reasons that have little to do with their stated purpose. Liquor prohibition aimed at the Natives bore little resemblance to the 1917 experiment. It was far more harsh, lasted far longer, and was based solely on race. Prohibition, when it came during the Great War, was the culmination of a mass movement towards reform, which had begun in early nineteenth-century North America. It was a response to the social dislocation brought on by rampant urbanization, industrialization and growth. This was not the case for the Natives. For them, prohibition sprang from two conflicting impulses. Originally, it was promoted as the natural outgrowth of eighteenth-century British imperialism — a benign desire to protect Aboriginal people from the evils and bad habits foisted upon them by encroaching civilization. But benevolence explains only part of the equation. As will become apparent, prohibition also proved very useful as a tool of intimidation to facilitate the expansion of white settlement and later, for social control.

For decades before wartime prohibition came to British Columbia in 1917, the province — and, later, Ottawa — had already been enforcing prohibition on a large segment of its own population. Before the arrival of Europeans in the late eighteenth century, alcoholic beverages were unknown in present-day British Columbia. At first, Natives regarded the new intoxicant with distaste and suspicion because of its strange taste and ability to incapacitate. When Captain Cook arrived at Nootka Sound in March 1778, he reported a complete absence of intoxicating liquors. When he offered inhabitants glasses of rum, the liquor was rejected as something unnatural and disgusting to the palate. But only fifteen years later the Spanish naturalist, José Mariano Moziño, reported that alcohol was well known among the Natives of Nootka Sound:

> They do not have any fermented beverage, and until they began to deal with Europeans they satisfied their thirst with nothing more than water. Since that time they have acquired quite an affection for wine, brandy, and beer, all of which they use excessively whenever there is someone who furnishes them liberally, but up to now the thought of procuring these liquors by means of commerce does not seem to have occurred to them.[2]

James Swan, one of the first settlers to arrive on the Oregon coast in the early 1850s, befriended the local Natives in Shoalwater Bay and recorded the following description of their first experience with alcohol fifty years earlier:

> They are all extravagantly fond of ardent spirits, and are not particular what kind they have, provided it is strong, and gets them drunk quickly. This habit they have acquired since the visit of Lewis and Clarke in 1805, for they state that they had not observed any liquors of an intoxicating kind used among any of the Indians west of the Rocky Mountains; and old Carcumcum has related to me the fact of her remembering the first time that any liquor was given to the Chenook Indians, and, from her description, I should think it was when Broughton went into the Columbia in the brig *Chatham*, for she said the *tyee*, or chief of the vessel, had *gold dollar* things, meaning epaulets, on his shoulders, and was in a man-of-war. They drank some rum out of a wine glass — how much she did not recollect; but she *did* recollect that they got drunk, and were so scared at the strange feeling that they ran into the woods and hid until they were sober. The rest, who did not get any rum, thought they had gone crazy, or had turned foolish. . . .[3]

During the late eighteenth century, unregulated traders from America, France, Spain, England and Russia aggressively pursued the "soft gold" of sea otter fur on the northwest coast. They cared nothing about permanent settlement and were happy to trade in both guns and liquor — with little interest in their long-term effects. After the turn of the century, the sea otter population crashed, and maritime trade fell into the hands of the Americans, who had a long history of trading alcohol to the Native peoples. John Jewitt, who was held captive in Nootka after his ship the *Boston* was overwhelmed in 1803, reported that she had over twenty puncheons (2,000 gallons) of rum on board for the fur trade.

The great trading companies and European nations that opened up western North America had doubts about alcohol as a trade good, but were hard pressed to find a viable alternative. Russians in Alaska made formal complaints to the Americans as early as 1808, but they were ignored. In 1812, the Montreal-based North West Company and John Jacob Astor's Pacific Fur Company agreed to stop providing the Natives with spirituous liquors. Sir George Simpson, overseas governor of the Hudson's Bay Company from 1826 to 1861, made a compact with the Russian American Company to eliminate the use of alcohol in the 1830s — unless competition by the "Boston peddlers" forced the company to do otherwise. In spite of these agreements and precautions, liquor traders quickly captured the bulk of the business.

Once rum became increasingly important as a trade good, there was no financial incentive to enforce the ban on alcohol. Traders evaded the restrictions by passing out drinks to seal the deal on a trade, or including a jug with payment for a job well done. Liquor quickly became an essential part of every trader's cargo on the northwest coast, with ten otter pelts being worth a bottle of whiskey (the Russians preferred trading vodka). One gallon of liquor could buy either a slave or two of the finest Hudson's Bay Company blankets.

Alcohol became esteemed by the Natives not only for its intoxicating powers, but also as a symbol of wealth and power. By the mid-nineteenth century, drink had become an intrinsic part of traditional gatherings such as potlatches and funerals. Unlike so many of the white man's "gifts," this one did not directly challenge the traditional way of life. In some ways it actually enhanced it:

> Drunkenness appeared as a desirable thing which outweighed its unpleasant consequences. It had preeminent value in the feast situation. The more intoxicated the guests became, the more conspicuously did they attest to the strength of the host's liquor, and to

their wealth which permitted them to be so lavish with hard-to-come-by whiskey and rum.[4]

In other words, liquor became a means of self-validation for the Native peoples, a rite of passage and a method of gaining access to the spirit world of shamans and the ancestors. It was also a way of thumbing one's nose at white authority and relieving boredom.

The strange customs, tools, foods and drink in the white settlements acted as a powerful magnet to the Native people; by the 1850s there were large permanent encampments next to Victoria and other Hudson's Bay trading stations. Many Natives around these posts seemed all too ready to give up their hardy, self-sufficient ways for a life of idleness and penury. Public displays of drunkenness were common among both races, and many of the new colonists, fresh from England, were quick to blame alcohol for the growing social dislocation in Native communities.

A brisk trade in Native women sold for spirits further scandalized the colony. The supposed connection between drink and immoral sexual relations with Natives was a common theme. In a letter to the editor of the *Nanaimo Gazette*, titled "Our Social Evil" and signed "Settler," the writer complained that the indiscriminate cohabitation of "white men" with "Indian women" was actually worse than trafficking in whiskey. Married people, he urged, "should be outraged" by such mixed unions, for it was "an insult to female delicacy" and would lead to the "total subversion of all moral restraint over the actions of the young." He proceeded to argue that the mixing of the races resulted in the white man being "invariably lowered in the social scale — becoming almost on a par with the people of his sensual and ignorant companion; while the only 'benefit' she receives by the connection is to be found in the facility by which she can obtain whiskey."[5] The "evil" was still further perpetuated, in his opinion, in the children resulting from such unions.

There was also the suspicion that Native wives were supplying spirits obtained by their husbands to other family members. "A large portion of the supply is obtained in this manner, and it will gradually go on increasing as the more open traffic becomes less likely to be carried on with safety."[6] Thus such marriages resulted, it was alleged, in the corruption of entire villages.

For the European colonists, the danger of "ardent spirits" was an old story. Cheap distilled liquor had been readily available since the early eighteenth century, and many knew first-hand the high social costs of spirits at home. Colonial authorities in British Columbia were quick to equate use with abuse when dealing with Natives. Drinking supposedly led inexorably to alcoholism, which in turn created an endless cycle of prostitution, domestic abuse, and social, economic and physical ruin. Some even blamed alcohol for the devastating disease epidemics then running rampant in the villages. Vivid exaggerations of drunkenness and debauchery among the Natives were a common theme in newspaper reports and accounts from visitors: "Any person having a knowledge of the Indian character must be aware of their proneness to commit the most desperate deeds when under the influence of the poisonous compound which passes with them for 'whiskey'. . . . It is the prolific source of all that is flagitious, and the radiating point of nearly all the misdemeanor or crime they commit." Such commentators often suggested that nothing short of the "wholesale annihilation of the Indians" would result from the sale of "tangle-leg."[7]

Of course, excessive use of alcohol was not limited to Natives. The colony of Vancouver Island was founded and governed by heavy drinkers. Robert Melrose, one of the first colonists to arrive in Victoria in the early 1850s, worked at the Hudson's Bay Company's Craigflower Farm, growing food for the colony. Drink apparently fascinated him, and his love for it was probably responsible for his own "failure to get on in the world." Melrose's diary described his first New Year's Day debauch in Victoria. It was undoubtedly penned while he was still tipsy:

> New Year's Day, a day above all days, for rioting in drunkenness, then what are we to expect of this young, but desperate Colony of ours; where dissipation is carried on to such extremities my reader will be expecting to find nothing in my Almanack, from Christmas, till past

the New Year, but such a one drunk, and another drunk, and so on; how different is the scene then what I must attribute the cause of all this, too, I must prescribe it to the good morals of the people; no! no! my friends, no such thing could be expected here; the grog-shops were drained of every sort of liquor, not a drop to be got for either love or money, had it been otherwise the case, there is no saying wither my small Almanack would have contained them or not; it would take a line of packet ships, running regular between here and San Francisco to supply this Island with grog, so great a thirst prevails amongst its inhabitants.[8]

In response to all this overindulgence, the colonial administrators began to look for more forceful ways to restrict access to alcohol for both settlers and Natives. In 1853, Governor Douglas asked his Executive Council to institute licensing fees: £100 for wholesale, and £125 for retail sales. The aim was to reduce consumption rather than raise revenue. Douglas' efforts were successful in bringing some order to the trade, but by 1864 there were 149 licensed outlets in Victoria — with only five policemen to keep them in line.[9]

It has long been claimed that North American Aboriginals are somehow more vulnerable to alcohol than those of other racial backgrounds, and more inclined to lose control when drinking. Certainly this belief was the justification for the maze of rules and regulations governing Aboriginal drinking that emerged after 1854. But the "firewater myth," as it has come to be called, has no basis in science. Books such as Joy Leland's *Firewater Myths: North American Indian Drinking and Alcohol Addiction,* Peter C. Mancall's *Deadly Medicine: Indians and Alcohol in Early America* and others, have demolished this much beloved racist stereotype. They conclude that North American Aboriginals respond in a variety of ways to alcohol, just like everyone else. No genetic trait has been found that predisposes them to drink, and Aboriginal people metabolize alcohol at the same rate that everyone else does. Interestingly enough, a strong predisposition towards alcohol can be found in some individuals from all races, but not in the races themselves. Almost everyone has a favourite caricature. Stories and jokes about drunken Irishmen, sodden Poles, potted Germans, befuddled Koreans, and wild-eyed Africans crazy with drink remain common fare. Yet none of this holds true for an entire people.

While it is true that there were some in early British Columbia, like the missionary William Duncan, who were genuinely concerned about the effect alcohol was having on British Columbia's Natives, there is a darker explanation for the province's first prohibition. Historian Nicholas Simons argues that the firewater myth was the construct of Europeans who needed stereotypes based on the "unalterable inferiority of Indians." Such views provided the rationale for confiscation of lands for settlement, while at the same time eliminating the need to look for other causes of the social dislocation in the Aboriginal community. He notes, "It becomes clear that the law was not simply a benign set of rules and regulations designed to protect individual interests, but rather, a coercive tool to diminish any opposition to economic plans of national policy."[10] In other words, the firewater myth was part and parcel of the myth that North America was a wilderness inhabited only by a small number of Natives who had no right to the land. As a presumably inferior race, the Natives had no right to block the claim to ownership and the redistribution of the land by European settlers.

Finally, after much discussion about the Native question, Douglas' Executive Council passed a law "prohibiting the gift or sale of Spirituous Liquors to Indians" in 1854 on the grounds that spirits were "manifestly injurious to the Native Tribes, endangering the public peace, and the lives and property of Her Majesty's Subjects." Beer was not an issue, because there were no breweries in the colony at this time. To be fair, members of the Vancouver Island Legislative Assembly raised questions about Native prohibition at that time. The issue occasionally surfaced in the local editorial pages. The *Nanaimo Gazette* first laid out the two possibilities: "Either the act for prohibiting the sale or gift of liquor to Indians must be repealed, allowing them to get their 'drinks' as other men, or else some strenuous effort must be made by the friends of the aborigines to bring the illicit trade going on among them to a stop."

But having set out the apparently reasonable option of allowing the Natives to drink like "other men," the *Gazette* renounced the idea and urged that the trade be shut down immediately, presumably because they were not in fact perceived as being like "other men."[11]

After the union of the two colonies of Vancouver Island and British Columbia in 1866, Native liquor laws were tightened even further. Penalties were increased to a $500 fine for selling, one third of which went to the informer. Police, customs and the Royal Navy were given greater rights of search. Ships from Washington to Alaska were required to produce a bill of lading on demand. If illicit liquor was found, the vessel and her cargo were forfeit, and the master faced a $1,000 fine. Persons possessing alcohol in a Native dwelling could be fined $500 and sentenced to six months in prison for a first offence — or to a year of hard labour for the second offence. Guilty children under the age of sixteen were whipped in private.[12]

In spite of the increasing penalties, Native liquor laws were routinely ignored and broken. A story in the *Victoria Daily Press* described the hellish scene at Cadboro Bay, after the Natives had been driven from their Victoria Reserve during the smallpox epidemic of 1862:

> *Indians at Cadboro Bay* — We learn from a farmer living in the neighbourhood, that a number of Hydah Indians are still encamped on this spot. The smallpox is raging amongst them, and several deaths occur daily from this cause. They have a tent erected apart from the rest of their dwellings, which they use for the purposes of a hospital. Drunkenness holds its sway amongst them, and they seem to possess any quantity of liquor. Two of the Elansah's brothers, and another Indian, called at the house of our informant on Sunday, and were very disorderly. They told him "that the police paid no attention to them, and they could get as much drink as they pleased." The families in the vicinity are in daily dread of outrage and disease from the proximity of these rascals. The Indians might just as well never have been driven from the Reserve, as half of their number come

into town daily. Out in such a place the settlers have no security from their depredations, and it devolves at once upon the authorities to expel them from a locality, in which no watch can be kept upon their movements.[13]

One can understand how these people, driven from their homes, and with smallpox raging among them, might well be searching for alcohol to ease their suffering.

Contempt for the law in both white and Aboriginal communities, combined with the effect of raw alcohol created a climate of anarchy and violence in outlying areas. In the fall of 1865, the Victoria schooner *Royal Charlie* arrived in Alaskan waters on a trading expedition with an illicit load of whiskey. Captain Thomas Goin, accompanied by a crew of three other whites and two young Native deckhands, was looking for furs. Although the men had been warned to be careful, business was slow. To bring in some customers, they offered a half-gallon of whiskey each to three local "Siwash" to spread the news. Several days later, a group of canoes arrived, which "appeared to be quite friendly." However, as the schooner got underway, a large canoe put out from shore, full of Kake "Indians all armed and half drunk." Five jumped on board, and the "chief" drew his dagger and cut the halyards on the mainsail, bringing it down. In the confusing melee that followed, four traders and two Natives died:

> Tom Goin, who was steering, immediately asked Tom the trader (name unknown) who was on deck with the rest, for his pistol, on getting which he fired at the Indian who cut the halyards, and wounded him in the wrist; the Indian then ran his knife through him; he [Goin] then took his revolver and struck the Indian on the head and also kicked him, then called out to John Cashman to bring up his gun and shoot him. The same Indian then stabbed Tom a second time and killed him. John Cashman then immediately killed the Indian. The four other Indians on seeing their chief killed went into their canoe, got their guns and fired, killing Tom the trader, John Cashman, and wounding the other man, Abbott who with the assistance of the two Indian boys belonging to the

schooner, got into the boat and went away. Abbott bled to death towards the evening and was landed on the beach by the boys, they then proceeded on to Stekin.[14]

In this "Heart of Darkness" world, debauchery and violence became a way of life for both sides.

While on the subject of Alaska, it should be noted that liquor prohibition was an even worse failure there than it was in British Columbia. In 1867, the U.S. Secretary of State, William Seward, arranged purchase of the huge territory from Russia, with the intent of ending the northwest rivalry between his country and Britain and Russia. Among the first acts of the new administration was the prohibition of alcohol in 1867 for both the Natives and settlers, and the establishment of a military occupation. In fact, the border area became a sieve for booze. But there was never any serious attempt to enforce the law, and the thriving market driven by both the Natives and settlers became an irresistible draw for bootleggers.

British Columbian vessels weighing less than 32 tons and travelling to Alaska paid no dues and were rarely inspected. Larger ships and steamers, which supplied the canneries, were granted special permits to pass through Alaskan waters, again without inspection. The myriad of canoes and smaller vessels were never required to file papers or be examined. It was a simple matter to pick up legal liquor in Hawaii, Victoria, Port Simpson or Mexico, and deliver it wherever one pleased. Smugglers altered labels, intimidated inspectors and handed out bribes with impunity.

The American Bureau of Customs seizure record for the Alaskan territory was the worst in the country, and the military occupiers were the worst offenders of all. With their privileged position, many left army service in Alaska far richer than when they arrived. The Klondike gold rush of the 1890s, which brought in tens of thousands of newcomers, ended any hope of continuing the prohibition. In 1899 Alaska moved to a licensing system, and the smuggler's boom suddenly collapsed.[15]

Back home in British Columbia, the Native peoples showed great ingenuity in evading the prohibition law by brewing their own "hoochinoo" out of molasses, flour, apples, berries, potatoes, yeast and hops. Tobacco, black chitons and wild elderberry juice were also often added. Tin containers and kelp tubing were juryrigged for distillation, creating vile and dangerous potions. Smuggled bottles of strange liquids with colourful names like Old Tom and Tarantula Juice became popular everywhere on the coast. These noxious concoctions were a potent mixture of alcohol, coal oil, red pepper and tobacco. Poisonings were common. The bootlegger's product was often no better. The price was high and the quality low. Liquor was almost always heavily diluted with water, and adulterated with such noxious substances as bluestone vitriol (a copper compound), nitric acid, vanilla extract, and perfumes like cologne, Jamaican Ginger and Florida Water.

Liquor was usually carried in a four-gallon molasses tin — a perfect cover — as molasses was one of the most popular trade items on the coast. The tins were simple to carry and hide, and easy to pitch over the side in an emergency. Spirits were preferred to beer or wine because the higher concentration of alcohol made it easier to transport. It is difficult to know how much illicit product was traded during this time. We do know that between 1858 and 1864, 336 people were arrested in the colony for selling "ardent spirits" to Natives. Another 240 people were convicted, and thousands of gallons of hard liquor were dumped into the sea.[16] The trade did not diminish over the years.

One of the most extraordinary proposals heard in Victoria was to remove the Native peoples altogether from white areas and banish them to "dry communities" far from the temptations of the trading posts. Just how this would have aided the assimilation of Natives into white culture was never made clear. Anyway, with thousands of uncooperative, sullen subjects, forceful removal was not practical. Indeed, the Native population far outnumbered the Europeans at this time. Nonetheless, the idea of a voluntary move was strongly favoured by the province's growing church missionary movement. Methodist, Anglican and other missionaries began arriving in the late 1850s with strong support from England. With a sincere desire to bring Christ to the heathen and improve the lot of the less fortunate, the missionary movement in England captured the imagination of tens of thousands, and by 1850 it had enormous support and financial resources to draw upon. The Church Missionary Society sent William Duncan to found the Metlakatla Christian Mission (near present-day Prince Rupert), while the Wesleyan Methodist missionary Thomas Crosby developed a similar mission at Port Simpson. The goal was not to establish an Aboriginal utopia, as has sometimes been claimed. Rather, it was to provide financial self-sufficiency, and demonstrate that the Native peoples could become skilled tradesmen and productive members of society without alcohol.

For its part, the colonial government did what it could to crack down on the coastal whiskey peddlers. The Royal Navy was enlisted as enforcer and, between 1860 and 1880, Her Majesty's ships intermittently scoured the coast for illicit traders. The navy was greatly aided by the new invention of steam power, which allowed pursuit into the smallest bay or estuary. One of the most successful of these liquor warriors was Commander John W. Pike of the paddle-sloop *Devastation*. Pike harassed booze sellers from Nanaimo to Russian Alaska, arresting suspects, confiscating vessels and dumping hundreds of gallons of "vile spirits" overboard. Governor Douglas described Pike's actions as "judicious and thorough," and the hardworking captain received special mention from the Lords of the British Admiralty. Not surprisingly, smugglers met this threat by organizing an extensive network of bootleggers, with regular schedules, hidden caches and forged papers. Much of the action took place near American and Russian territory, which provided refuge from British warships. Alcohol was usually sold right off the boat — cash and carry only.

Inevitably, the hard-nosed tactics on the part of the Royal Navy led to a number of ugly confrontations between the Native peoples and the gunboats. In 1866, Captain Nicholas Edward Turnour of the Royal Navy's steam corvette *Clio* moved to halt the local whiskey trade in northern waters. After chasing and seizing several whiskey schooners near the Nass River, Turnour was informed that liquor was freely available in Kitimat and that a Christian Native had been murdered there. A crew member described for the *British Colonist* the Royal Navy's brutal method of confiscating liquor and rounding up the usual suspects:

> On Sunday we got out the launch, pinnace, and two cutters and pulled, as only British seamen can pull, for the village. On sighting it [the pinnace] ran on shore, and in a few minutes all hands formed in companies opposite the principal lodge of the village, which latter apparently covered about a half mile of land. The Marines marched up to the house of the only white resident, who is well known by the name of "Frank," who keeps a store there, and who on the entrance of the Lieutenant and two or three marines, suddenly found himself prisoner on the old charge of whiskey selling; but as the tribe had had information of our coming . . . we could find no liquor among them. We proceeded from house to house, hunting various men who were "wanted" in connection with the crime alleged and who gave us much trouble from their natural desire to remain where they were. After some time . . . many high words were uttered, and as coolly answered by the significant appearance of the bright ends of bayonets and the sharp click of the rifle, and the disarming of one unlucky animal with a short musket loaded and cocked for the especial benefit of the First Lieutenant.[17]

All of the accused smugglers were brought on board the *Clio* and tried by William Duncan of the Metlakatla Christian Mission. Duncan, an appointed magistrate, was merciless, handing out severe penalties unheard of in Victoria. The three captains each received fines of £600 to £800 or six to eight years in jail, and their mates lesser sentences.[18] Outraged, the prisoners complained of the rough and unfair treatment they had received, and vowed to appeal. It was the right decision, for on their return to Victoria the verdicts were all quashed, and everyone went free.

For all its zeal in arresting Natives suspected of selling liquor, the Royal Navy had a limited number of ships on Pacific Station, and its resources were thinly stretched. It was expensive for Britain to maintain naval strength in far-away British Columbia. Moreover, the need to keep the United States at bay, maintain domestic peace, suppress slavery, and apprehend criminals competed with the anti-alcohol patrols. In the settlements and trading posts, administrators regularly complained that there was no funding to support any real police control. The legislature consistently refused to appropriate the necessary funds, and often dealt leniently with those caught breaking the rules. There were only five overworked police constables in the colony, and they needed witnesses for a successful prosecution. Furthermore, the province was becoming more dependent on alcohol for its economic well-being. Importation, production, transportation, sale, and taxes generated jobs and money that were not easily replaced. There was simply no political will to enforce liquor prohibition against the Natives.

Enforcement was further stymied by the casual racism of the times. His Honour W.H. Franklyn of Nanaimo advised his police court that when it came to apprehending criminals, ". . . it was not the province of Indian policeman to arrest white men in an illegal act. They should hurry off to the nearest place where a white policeman is stationed and there lodge an information; but not on any account to attempt making an arrest themselves."[19] This effectively granted immunity to white bootleggers, and it raised questions about the seriousness of the colonial authorities in ending the trade.

Further consolidation took place after the province joined the Dominion of Canada in 1871. In addition to taking on British Columbia's debt and providing generous railroad subsidies, the federal government passed the Indian Act in 1876, which granted Ottawa enormous powers over all of Canada's First Nations. In exchange for tax exemptions, a special status was created for those Natives listed on band rolls. This led to a peculiar dual system of government, with the provincial government having jurisdiction over non-Indians, while federal laws governed status Indians. Both provincial and federal governments colluded in treating their

Aboriginal subjects like unruly children. Natives, other than war veterans, could not vote in provincial elections until 1949, and federal elections until 1960. They could not attend public schools, could not homestead a piece of property, were deprived of public services on their reserves, and suffered under one of the most oppressive alcohol prohibitions ever imposed.

The laws governing Natives and alcohol actually redefined and widened the definition of who was "Indian." Under the Indian Act, Indians were those indigenous people who had signed a treaty with the Crown as well as the direct male descendants of such people. But this definition was difficult to apply in British Columbia, which had long insisted that Aboriginal rights did not exist, and had signed almost no treaties. Liquor laws were amended over the years, and the statutes became increasingly inclusive. They forbade sale to "any Indian or non-treaty Indian, or any person male or female who is reputed to belong to a particular Indian band, or who follows the Indian mode of life." This kind of vague blurring of race and lifestyle gave authorities enormous power over the Aboriginal population and their relations.[20]

Indeed, that was part of the strategy. People of mixed race or "half-breeds" could legally possess liquor, and were often accused of providing Natives with alcohol. Sociology professor Renisa Mawani, has argued that the laws governing Native drinking in British Columbia were directed primarily at this group.[21] Discrimination was further entrenched in the 1921 Government Liquor Act, which denied British Columbia liquor permits to those who fell under the jurisdiction of the Indian Act. Again, during the Second World War, when it became apparent that Natives were using illegal liquor permits, the province's Liquor Control Board (LCB) convinced the federal government to stamp "Indian" on the back of national registration certificates. These certificates were required whenever a person applied for a liquor permit for store purchases.

Both bartenders and owners could be charged along with Natives, and those serving beer often had to make difficult snap decisions based on unreliable standards of behaviour and appearance.

Police adopted a sniff test, where they smelled the breath of suspects for evidence of intoxication. Mexicans and others with a dark skin hue risked eviction or arrest in a bar, club or liquor store. To remedy the confusion, the LCB suggested that individuals under question could obtain an "official letter" indicating that they were not Indian under the meaning of the Indian Act.

There was one bizarre option open to Natives who wanted a drink legally: they could become "enfranchised." That is, they could give up their status Indian designation and become Canadian citizens. Between 1857 and 1940, fewer than 500 bothered with this bureaucratic hurdle.[22] The double standard created a nightmare for enforcement. When an enfranchised Indian was drinking with his status Indian friends, sorting out who could legally drink and who could not became impossible. The experience of the Second World War brought matters to a head. Thousands of Native veterans returned home to find the rules unchanged. Canada's First Nations people were in the humiliating position of having fought valiantly on the battlefields of both World Wars, but were unable to enjoy a beer in a pub with their comrades back in Canada. The laws reinforced the feeling of being second-class citizens. Privileges routinely accorded to everyone else were being denied to Natives simply because of their race. With the change of attitudes brought about by World War Two, even many abstainers were now opposed to the idea that Natives should be singled out for special treatment when it came to alcohol. Ironically, the struggle for equal liquor rights quickly moved to the forefront of the wider struggle for a change in the status quo. Colonial prohibitionists must have been rolling in their graves.

Mary John of the Stoney Creek Reserve in North Central British Columbia remembers how it was that Natives were given the right to drink and buy alcohol:

> So many men from Stoney Creek and reserves all across Canada had served overseas in the armed forces, in England, Scotland, France, Italy and Germany. They drank in canteens, as they called the beer parlors, just like white soldiers. When those who survived the war returned to Canada, the Native ex-servicemen found that under the

Indian Act they were still forbidden to drink alcohol anywhere in their own country. . . . People say that it was the returned soldiers who brought about a change in the Indian Act.[23]

Two British Columbia groups, the Native Brotherhood of British Columbia (founded 1931), and Andrew Paull's smaller North American Indian Brotherhood began to agitate for changes in the Indian Act. In 1946, the first issue of the Native Brotherhood's newspaper *The Native Voice* clearly spelled out their complaints:

> We suffer as a minority race and as ward, or minors without a voice in regard to our own welfare. We are prisoners of a controlling power in our own country — a country which has stood up under the chaos of two world wars, beneath the guise of democracy and freedom, yet keeping enslaved a Native people in their own home land. . . . Our Dominion is not in a position to point a finger of scorn at the treatment meted out by countries toward their people, until she liberates her own original and subjected race.[24]

Once *The Native Voice* pointed out that Canada was not in a position to point a finger of scorn at the racism of Germany and other countries because it had not yet "liberated" its own "original and subjected race," the federal government had no choice but to respond sympathetically. In fact, world attitudes towards race and colour were undergoing a marked change after the Second World War, and the idea of a two-tiered apartheid society was meeting increasing disfavour. The great European powers were being systematically driven out of their colonies in Asia and Africa, Blacks were demanding equal rights in the United States, and the horrific racism of Hitler's final solution was on everyone's mind. The Cold War, with each side loudly proclaiming the superiority of their system over the other, made the Indian Act seem even more an anachronism.

Yet even with all this world attention to the evils of racism, paradoxically the authorities in British Columbia continued to bear down on Native drinking, particularly in public beer parlours. The Mounties actually stepped up enforcement in the mid-1940s, posting a constable to patrol Vancouver's beer parlours for Native drinkers.[25] At times their enthusiasm for enforcement conflicted with the more moderate Liquor Control Board, whose officials felt that the police were going out of their way to punish Native drinkers by entrapping operators and beer parlour workers. In a pattern that has become familiar over the years; the enforcers of drug laws often became the strongest boosters of those laws. Maintaining the laws against Aboriginal drinking had become an end in itself — a form of bureaucratic preservation. As Natives pushed harder for equal treatment, they met with stronger resistance from police.

Extensive bootlegging continued, with Natives in remote areas trucking in bulk orders through compliant white and Chinese shop owners. For more modest needs, taxi drivers could usually be depended upon to provide a bottle — for an outrageous twenty-five dollars for a fifth. In Port Alberni it was not uncommon for whites to supply the first drinks to Natives free of charge, then demand exorbitant sums for more. Hope, with a population of fifteen hundred, furnished more than forty bootleggers to service nearby Native communities.[26]

In the spring of 1946, Ottawa set up a joint committee of the House and Senate to review the Indian Act. Individuals and groups from both races appeared before the committee for over two years, and almost all urged an end to Native prohibition. The committee findings in 1951 were to have far-reaching effects beyond the alcohol debate, and marked a watershed. The long promoted idea of "assimilation" of Natives into the Canadian mainstream was beginning to be discredited, replaced by an acceptance of their unique culture and right to live as they chose. At the same time it was understood that Aboriginals should have the same rights as any other Canadian citizen. In mid-1951, the Indian Act was revised to allow Natives to drink beer "upon any premises where any intoxicants may lawfully be sold and consumed." Each province would have to give its approval, and British Columbia granted assent in December 1951.

Unfortunately, the final version of the draft amendment changed the wording slightly to "for consumption in a public place in accordance with a law of the province." The British Columbia Liquor Control Board chose to interpret this narrowly to mean hotel beer parlours only. Government liquor stores and clubs, including veterans' associations, remained off-limits to Natives because they were not deemed "public places." One small change in the wording would have solved everything, but it was never made. This failure was probably due, in part, to traditional fears of mixing firewater and Indians. Unlike beer parlours, private clubs had been allowed to sell hard liquor to patrons since 1947.[27] Nonetheless, the right to drink in a beer parlour marked a major accomplishment for Aboriginal rights.

There had always been considerable disagreement in the Native community about the dangers of alcohol, but most regarded the *partial* lifting of restrictions as an insult. One Native editor described it as "asinine,"[28] and Andrew Paull called it a "trap" because it was still illegal to be drunk on a reserve. "How is the Indian to sober up after drinking on licensed premises which are near the reservation? Indians should have all privileges under B.C. liquor laws."[29] Even the mainstream press had its doubts. Roy W. Brown's column in the *Vancouver Sun* described the limitations as cowardly:

> By a half-baked decision contained in an order-in-council passed at Victoria, the authorities obviously think they are conferring a favor — something in the nature of a new freedom — on the native population. That it is regarded by the recipients as nothing of the kind is shown by the quick and unanimous rejection by a group of chiefs of coastal Indians.... Over a period of several hundreds of years in Canada, especially during the last half-century, when we should have reached an age of more sense and enlightenment, we have been withholding rights from the native brother that long ago should have been accorded him.[30]

Nevertheless, British Columbia became the first province after Prince Edward Island to extend "tavern privileges" to First Nations peoples. The grand opening on December 15, 1951, created a flurry of concern. The *Victoria Daily Times* blared, "Vendors braced for Invasion"[31]; and the next day, the *Vancouver Sun* proclaimed,

"Indians in Pubs Worry to Police."[32] The changeover, however, turned out to be uneventful. There was no grand rush to the beer parlours, and the Natives who did come to partake "behaved in a very gentlemanly manner."[33] Not surprisingly, the new patrons appeared conscious that their behaviour was being closely monitored, and were consequently quiet and orderly. Not a single case of drunkenness was reported by authorities. In spite of the peaceful transition, the Mounties argued against the change, with the province's assistant commissioner observing darkly, "wherever there are Indians in quantity, close to beer parlours, considerable damage is being done, not only from a general but an economic standpoint."[34]

In 1952, the political complexion changed in British Columbia with the election of W.A.C. Bennett and his dry-leaning Social Credit Party. Although he was a non-drinker, Bennett appointed a commission to examine the province's liquor laws and make recommendations. The result was a new liquor act in 1954, which, among other things, designated restaurants, cocktail lounges and some nightclubs as licensed public places where hard liquor could be served by the glass. Theoretically, Natives could visit these establishments, but did so only infrequently because of high prices, an unfriendly atmosphere and "outright discrimination." Military service clubs remained closed to them.

In 1956, Ottawa amended the Indian Act again. Provisions were made for three stages of "development" that would end the ban on alcohol. The first permitted a province to petition the federal government to allow Natives to drink in a "public place." This had been in effect in BC since 1951. The second was to allow a province to petition Ottawa to allow hard liquor sales off the reserve. If stage two was successfully completed, stage three would permit individual bands to hold a referendum to decide about sale and consumption on the reserve.

While all of this sounded like progress, matters moved with agonizing slowness. In early 1957, the Social Credit Attorney-General Robert Bonner explained that the government was still studying the three-stage system and that the "Indians themselves are quite divided." As late as 1961, veterans of the Army, Navy and Air Force tried unsuccessfully to use the Canadian Bill of Rights to force the province to open service clubs to all of British Columbia's veterans.

It took a violent street riot to restart the process. The "Centennial Riot" of August 2, 1959, began as a small street altercation in Prince Rupert, which was celebrating its 100th birthday. When police tried to arrest three Natives, the crowd of bystanders exploded, battling with the RCMP and each other for two hours. Rocks and bottles were thrown, and police lobbed twenty-five teargas bombs into the unruly crowd. Eventually eighty people were arrested and thirty-nine charged — twenty-four of them were Natives. There was considerable sympathy for those charged, as one-third of Prince Rupert's 10,000 residents were Natives, giving the city the highest concentration of First Nations people in the province. Although the press tried to blame anonymous "mobsters" for the riot, Mayor Peter Lester, Native spokesman Harold Sinclair, the Prince Rupert Labour Council and others called for a Royal Commission to examine law enforcement in the city and the "alleged discrimination against Native people." In September the city council passed a resolution calling for full liquor rights for the First Nations people.[35]

The Bennett government, however, continued to stall, claiming that future changes would have to be initiated by Ottawa and the First Nations themselves. In 1960, Frank Calder and the Nisga'a Tribal Council came up with a creative solution to the impasse. They directly petitioned the federal government to ignore the second stage of the three-tiered plan, and allow Natives an immediate vote on reserve drinking. The Indian Affairs Branch expressed concern about this unusual approach. If some bands voted themselves dry and others wet, it would be impossible to sort out who could drink and who could not, and this might actually increase feelings of discrimination. But something had to be done to break the impasse. Indian Affairs decided to give the province sixty days notice to respond to news of the impending vote.

British Columbia's Attorney-General, Robert Bonner, cynically lambasted the federal government for the "fantastic rigmarole" surrounding the liquor laws, while amending the provincial Liquor Act in March 1961 to place the burden of changing the law and its consequences solely on Ottawa. The Bennett government did not, however, directly challenge the Nisga'a petition, and four Nass River communities voted overwhelming for liquor two months later.[36] Others soon followed. By May 1962, Attorney-General Bonner was telling law enforcement officers to take a "very generous attitude" towards Natives and liquor. On July 1, he announced that the LCB had been instructed to stop enforcing the liquor laws against the First Nations people. Bonner explained the change as a death blow to bootlegging. He observed that "the only people injured by this will be that shadowy band of people who over the years have been supplying liquor to Indians clandestinely."[37] Strangely, the Indian Affairs Branch continued to insist that the wet/dry votes continue on the reserves. By April 1963, ninety bands had requested the ballot; and of the forty-seven who had already voted, only three wanted a dry reserve.[38]

Most seemed happy with the changes. Guy Williams, president of the Native Brotherhood, was delighted. He noted that his group had been fighting to obtain Native liquor rights for twenty-five years, and that 80 percent of the Indians in jail were there for liquor offences. Magistrate Roderick Haig-Brown of Campbell River repeated the statement he had given in 1958:

> Many Indians appear in my court every year. They are rarely charged with anything more serious than having bought or drunk liquor. But an Indian case is never trivial. Indians come to court on these charges with a sense of injustice and discrimination. They are right.... It is not simply a question of liquor, but of freedom, and human dignity that belongs with freedom. I am ashamed every time it is the duty of my court to punish Indians for something that is a crime only for them.[39]

But there were several politicians and officials such as Magistrate Lionel Beevor-Potts of Nanaimo, who remained opposed, commenting that "99% of trouble with Indians was attributable to liquor, and less, not more, should be made available to them."[40]

In sum, the evidence suggests that liquor prohibition for British Columbia's First Nations was a disastrous failure. Not only was it patently racist and unenforceable, it had a number of other negative effects that are rarely considered. Prohibition actually encouraged the abuse of alcohol in Native communities. Drinking became a symbol of solidarity and rising political consciousness. Violators tended to be treated as heroes rather than pariahs. "Drinking the forbidden liquor thus became for the Indian an act of aggression against white authority and at the same time a protest against imputation of inferiority explicit in the Indian Act and implicit in daily social interaction between whites and Indians."[41]

Prohibition for the Natives also tended to increase the potency of the alcohol sold. A very high concentration of alcohol means that the container can be small, making it easier to transport, hide, sell and drink from. Studies have shown that this pattern applies to many illicit drugs, and it was repeated during the 1917 prohibition. Make something illegal, and the bootleg variety will invariably be stronger (if possible) than what is usually consumed. For alcohol in particular, the stronger percentage greatly adds to the danger, as the drug becomes far more addictive and dangerous in high-proof concentrations.

Native prohibition also encouraged faster drinking — to facilitate prompt destruction of the evidence. Being caught drunk and empty-handed by the authorities was far less serious than being nabbed with a couple of full bottles. Even after the beer parlours were opened to the First Nations in 1951, the half-baked policies actually encouraged rapid drinking. Mary John observed, "People would drink as much as they could before closing time, because they knew that once they left the beer parlor, the only place they could drink was in some back alley or beside the railway tracks."[42]

It is difficult to gauge the true legacy of liquor for British Columbia's First Nations. The early years of settlement were the worst. One writer estimated in 1902 that more than 100,000 people died as a direct result of alcohol consumption between 1858 and 1870.[43] Yet, these early estimates concerning the death toll are misleading because many saw excessive use of drink as the exclusive cause of cultural disintegration when it was really a symptom. Most observers choose to ignore the ferocious European epidemics, the heavy-handed confiscation of lands, and the forced abandonment of a traditional lifestyle. Moreover, drink was an entirely new drug for Northwest Natives, and they had no idea of its allure and danger. These other factors all contributed greatly to the epidemic of alcoholism that haunted the Native shantytowns surrounding white settlements. As happens today, regardless of race, the poorest communities under the greatest stress suffer the worst rate of substance abuse.

The early prohibition of liquor for Natives in British Columbia was a surreal dress rehearsal for the later wartime prohibition in the province. For whatever reason, British Columbia's prohibitionists of the early twentieth century made little attempt to assess and learn from the Native experience. If they had, they could have saved themselves much trouble.

CHAPTER 3

REFORM, THE SOCIAL GOSPEL AND PREMIER RICHARD McBRIDE

IN THE EARLY YEARS OF the twentieth century, British Columbia was undergoing vast changes, with the population doubling every decade. In 1891 there were 98,200 people; in 1901, 178,700; in 1911, 392,500; and by 1921, 526,600. The sudden influx must have been mind-boggling. Old-timers who had arrived only twenty years earlier looked back on the nineteenth century with nostalgia, as the province changed beyond recognition before their eyes. New inventions like the telephone, automobile, mechanized farm equipment, and the introduction of electricity rapidly transformed the province. A majority of the population claimed "British" as their ethnic origin, but there were also thousands of Chinese, Hawaiians, Ukrainians, Poles, Germans, Japanese, Black Americans and others. By 1910, one in ten of Vancouver's population of 100,000 was Asian, and there was continuing tension over jobs and wages.

Most of the population worked at mining, fishing and logging. Others toiled at building infrastructure: railroads, bridges, roads and buildings. Intense activity characterized the summer months, followed by periods of boredom during the long, dark winters. Men headed off to work in isolated camps operated by impersonal business concerns where the company bosses exercised tremendous power. They provided the jobs and accommodations but they also sold essential food, drink and supplies through the company store and bar at high prices. Working conditions were harsh, and organized labour was harassed and harried by the police and business. With the province's strong sense of worker solidarity, waves of strikes paralyzed the province in 1900, 1911 and 1912. In December 1900 there were about one hundred unions in the province, and by 1903 that number had more than doubled.

All over North America, people watched their familiar world being transformed by the surging population and rapid economic growth. These changes brought a higher standard of living, but they also unleashed a host of unexpected social problems. Poverty, bad working conditions, homelessness, alienation, unemployment and much else besides demonstrated the darker side of the industrial revolution. A strong religious revival in the mid-nineteenth century led Methodists, Presbyterians, Roman Catholics and others to ask: Who is my brother's keeper? They reacted against the harsh Darwinian determinism of the times and embraced the Social Gospel movement. Religion was not only about saving one's soul; it also involved a call for social justice. Man was obligated to become an activist, struggling to improve the lives of others less fortunate, rather than to live a life of passive acceptance. Religious writers of the time argued for a life of involvement in the community:

> Abundance of Life is to be attained, not through any brute struggle on the part of men or nations in accord with some biological law of survival of the fittest, but through mutual service in accord with the principles of a higher law, the law of human brotherhood which finds its sublime expression in Christian sacrifice and love.[1]

The old view of spiritual redemption found only in heaven was replaced by a vision of salvation on earth. According to such religious activists, evil in the world was due to bad environment rather than personal defect. Capitalism, the quest for profit, animal competition and the autocratic regimes of government and industry had created intolerable living and working conditions. The perverted system needed to be replaced by something different based on Christian principles.

For believers in the Social Gospel, radical change in society was not only possible but necessary. Many of these reformers were also devout socialists who had no problem reconciling their socialism with Christianity. E.A. Partridge, an early twentieth-century prairie radical, once observed: "One must take your love of God, which in its practical form is love of your neighbour, into politics." Practical religion is to be employed each day, he argued, but especially for election day when committed social Christians could purge "those who represent the most heartless and selfish interests of the race...."[2]

The obvious dangers posed by alcohol made it an easy target, and for those looking for simple solutions, prohibition seemed to provide all the answers. Drink could be associated legitimately with many evils, including poverty, accidents, unemployment, insanity, sickness, prostitution, sloth and death. If government could legislate to protect children, workers and animals from abuse, should not it also be able to protect citizens from the dangers of demon booze?

Many turned to the trendy new discipline of "science" to buttress their argument, but science proved an unreliable ally in the war against alcohol because it could not make up its own mind. Ninety percent of doctors still prescribed alcohol as medicine, yet three-quarters believed that total abstinence would create a healthier society.[3] For some, dependence on drink was seen as a moral failure to restrain oneself — a "disease of the will." This conveniently placed the blame squarely on the victim, and obscured the connection between social problems and the overwhelming

▲ Lieutenant-Governor Frederick Seymour, c. 1865, left, at his New Westminster official residence, demonstrating "how we passed time on board the *Oregon Steamer*" from Portland, Oregon to Vancouver Island.
(COURTESY BC ARCHIVES, E-03969)

▲ William Hogarth's "Gin Lane" (1750/1751). Hogarth engraved his companion pieces "Gin Lane" and "Beer Street" to show the "dredfull consequences of gin drinking," after gin as a distilled liquor had become cheap and readily available in England.

▲ William Hogarth's "Beer Street" (1750/1751) shows how beer is an "invigorating liquor" which makes everything "joyous and thriving," where "Industry and Jollity go hand in hand."

▶ Hootsnahu (Village of the Whiskey Makers), c. 1880s. After the arrival of the Europeans, First Nations people used kelp tubing and molasses tins for distilling home-made alcohol. (COURTESY BC ARCHIVES, G-09230)

▲ Alcohol, secreted in anonymous barrels and tins, became one of the many "gifts" distributed at potlatches. Alert Bay Potlatch, c. 1910. (COURTESY BC ARCHIVES, F-04182)

▶ The first stores that opened for business in a new municipality were invariably shops selling wines and liquors. Kennedy Flat, Leech River near Sooke, c. 1866. (COURTESY BC ARCHIVES, A-04474)

▲ Taku City near Atlin. A teeming tent city complete with a saloon, c. 1906. (COURTESY BC ARCHIVES, D-09362)

▶ Waiting for the mail in front of the Bucket of Blood, c. 1890s, in Fairview in the Okanagan. Saloons were the hub of social life in early BC. (COURTESY BC ARCHIVES, F-06572)

changes overtaking the province. For others, alcoholism was seen as a form of insanity — a "psychosis" or "neurosis" in the parlance of the budding field of psychiatry. The addiction was caused by a pre-existing malady in the central nervous system, triggered by the alcohol. The blame was first attributed to emotional or physical trauma, and later conveniently ascribed to inheritance. Your parent's bloodline decided your fate in life. This pseudo-scientific explanation fitted in perfectly with the racial and class prejudices of the times. Treatments became fashionable for those who could afford them. Inebriate asylums were organized to keep people from temptation while providing constant medical attention. Long soaks in a warm bath (hydrotherapy), and injections of bi-chloride of gold were highly favoured. But the medical community remained hopelessly divided about the causes of alcohol addiction, and failed to come up with any consistent consensus for treatment.

While the Protestant-based Social Gospel and temperance movement surged in the rest of Canada, it remained weak in British Columbia. This was largely a factor of religious demographics. People from England made up 59 percent of the population in 1901 and 75 percent by 1921. By 1921, statistics showed that 30.8 percent of the population identified themselves as Anglicans and 23.5 percent as Scottish Presbyterians.[4] No other province in Canada contained such a high proportion of immigrants from the British Isles, and their tolerance of alcohol consumption carried considerable weight with those who made the rules. Most regarded the anti-liquor fanaticism of the Methodists and others with scepticism, even disdain. The Anglican General Synod in London voiced the following prescient warning in 1902: "In remedying those evils [of drink] in one direction, we must be careful lest we create others probably as great in another. Stringent laws often defeat their purpose, and cannot be enforced unless they are supported by the hearty cooperation of all classes."[5]

For most Anglicans and many Presbyterians, moderating one's drinking habits was the solution to intemperance, not a heavy-handed prohibition. They argued that both the Bible and Jesus preached moderation rather than abstinence. Christ himself drank wine, turned water into wine for his followers, and promised that they would all drink wine together in heaven. In Proverbs, the advice was to "Give strong drink unto him that is ready to perish, and wine unto those that be of heavy heart. Let him drink and forget his poverty, and remember his misery no more." (The "strong drink" in this passage probably did not refer to "ardent spirits," but rather to wine diluted by two parts water.) There is little biblical evidence to suggest that God despised alcohol.

Another factor that limited the influence of the temperance movement in British Columbia was the loose and forgiving frontier standard of behaviour in the province. The western province had long had a reputation in the rest of Canada for being unbridled and wide open — similar in many ways to the American Wild West. Authorities openly tolerated a level of public drunkenness and prostitution that was not acceptable in the east. Historians have often asked why. Perhaps part of the explanation lies with the demographics of the province. There was a decided dearth of women available for the thousands of male workers. The ratio of European men to women in the province was 148 to 100 in 1881, 177 to 100 in 1901, and 127 to 100 in 1921. Given these figures, a normal life with wife and family was unusual, and the lack of female society and family life helped set the tone of early twentieth-century British Columbia. With a paucity of women, society came to be influenced by rough, young, highly mobile working class males, upon whose labour the province depended. Given this imbalance, it is not surprising that prostitution and liquor consumption were so popular. These distractions kept the economy healthy and, without them, it would have been difficult to attract the workers necessary for steady economic growth.

Red-light districts could be found in most towns, and constables routinely collected protection money of five to eight dollars a month from ladies of the night. In Vancouver, notorious Dupont Street hosted forty-one houses with 153 girls in 1906.[6] Prostitution, like alcohol, was accepted as part of the price for economic development. As long as there were no complaints and the women followed the informal rules set by local wives, police left the girls alone. The visibility of garishly dressed ladies caused problems in smaller communities, where they were put under curfew and restricted to certain areas — but rarely banished. In prosperous cities like Victoria, high-priced harlots rode shamelessly around town in expensive carriages, dressed in the latest fashion.

Even in the rest of Canada, after some initial successes, the temperance movement began to bog down. Anti-liquor groups united in the 1870s to form the nation-wide Dominion Alliance for the Total Suppression of the Liquor Traffic, which took a lead in lobbying the federal government for the Local Option. The Local Option was an attempt to give local municipalities greater control over liquor sales by allowing the electorate to petition for a vote on the banning of liquor sales in a municipality. A simple majority could decide the issue, with another vote following three years after — if the electorate wished. In 1878, the federal government finally agreed to implement the idea, and enacted the Canada Temperance Act, or Scott Act, but it soon ran into jurisdictional trouble in the courts.

The British North America Act had granted the provinces control of the licensing of saloons and taverns; it remained silent about who regulated and taxed the transportation, manufacture and sale of liquor. Revenues and patronage from these activities were enormously valuable, and within a few years every province had moved to fill this vacuum with its own laws, fees and taxes. Covetously watching the money roll in, the federal government moved to take liquor powers away from the provinces. A number of lengthy court cases followed, in which federal and provincial judges tried to sort out the complicated question of provincial/federal liquor jurisdiction. In frustration, Ottawa turned the whole question over to the Judicial Committee of the Privy Council, the highest court in the land. The privy councillors carefully divided jurisdiction, giving something to everyone. The provinces had the right to oversee retailing and were given the power to act within their own borders. Ottawa was given jurisdiction over manufacture and inter-provincial distribution. Although this resolved the dispute, it offended the prohibitionists, because it legitimized liquor. It also laid the groundwork for future problems.

By the 1870s, however, a new element in the struggle was making its appearance which would give the temperance movement additional support. Women were organizing and confronting the liquor interests head on, while demanding a greater say at home and in government. This led to noisy demonstrations, prayer meetings and, in some cases, the physical destruction of saloons and their liquor. In the United States, thousands of bars were vandalized or shut down, and the organizers held a victory convention in Cleveland, Ohio, where, in 1874, they formally united as the Woman's Christian Temperance Union (WCTU). The leaders saw their role in society as "organized mother love." Although they dedicated themselves primarily to suppressing the liquor traffic, other noble causes assumed increasing importance.

Under Frances A. Willard, the WCTU reached out to the world, adopting a "do everything policy" that encompassed a wide range of social causes. Forty-five departments were set up, each with its own set of responsibilities: the Department of Health and Hygiene, which worked against narcotics, tobacco and alcohol in patent medicines; the Department of Social Purity, which called for stiffer penalties against white slavers and the rehabilitation of prostitutes; the Department of Purity in Art and Literature, which railed against nudity in art, anatomical drawings and circus side shows; and the Department for the Suppression of Sabbath Desecration, which wanted to ban all activities but church on Sundays. The WCTU also strongly supported women's suffrage, recognizing that the ballot box was a key component in advancing their platform.

As part of the WCTU's program, "Scientific temperance instruction" was heavily touted in the schools as early as 1886. The WCTU's Temperance Publishing Association in Illinois churned out a multitude of texts, readers and pamphlets, many of which found their way to Canada. Pseudo-scientific texts like *The Temperance Teachings of Science*, by A.B. Palmer, became a mind-numbing staple for most schoolchildren. The propaganda was invariably in favour of total abstinence.

By 1883 the WCTU had gone global, with branches in fifty-one countries, including Canada, Japan, England and Argentina. In June of that year, Miss Frances Willard was in the Northwest on a promotional tour for the WCTU, and made an appearance in Victoria. She had a charismatic presence. Slender, boyish, and intense, with carrot-coloured hair, Willard enchanted audiences. The following rapturous account of her appearance in Portland Oregon, shortly before her arrival in Victoria vividly imparts the flavour of her appearance:

> At the reception tendered to Miss Frances A. Willard last night at the M.E. Church, on Taylor Street, there was the largest and deeply interested assemblage ever collected together in an auditorium where sincere and fervent audiences are most wont to gather, to be thrilled by the power of a woman's voice pleading the cause of temperance. There was assembled a multitude that filled every nook and corner of the spacious church. They crowded the seats and filled the aisles and gallery, and hung around the altar within the railing, so eager were they to witness the graceful and fervent expressions about to be extended to this devoted woman worker. The wreaths and baskets of flowers; a splendid arch of solid green rising over the pulpit and bedecked about the base with roses, and surmounted with a dove, the white, outstretched wings of which seemed TYPICAL OF THE CHRISTIAN SPIRIT that hovered over and blessed the noble woman in her sacred work. After remarks from several gentlemen, Miss Willard was introduced and began an address that enchained the eye and the ear. She was very rapid, but graceful in delivery, and her thoughts found utterance, without hesitation or delay. She pictured her home life and the unselfish spontaneous desire that impelled her to start out to the relief of suffering humanity, without money or thought of the morrow, but the Lord had always provided.[7]

Absolute and complete prohibition was essential for women, Willard urged, because "the greatest harm done by alcohol is to people who never taste it." The women, she assured the audience, were the ones who bore the real brunt of alcohol abuse.

Of course, women drank, too, but if they were respectable, they sipped patent "medicine" — which was not considered liquor, although the medicine might include Rexall's Rheumatic Remedy with 18 percent alcohol, Hooker's Wigwam Tonic with 20.7 percent, Lydia Pinkham's Vegetable Compound with 20 percent, Hall's Great Discovery with 43 percent, Hostelter's Bitters with 46 percent, and Hamlin's Wizard Oil, with an incredible 65 percent alcohol.[8]

Willard presented her audience with "A Declaration of Principles" which demanded members sign the pledge for total abstinence and agree that government should enact laws to suppress the liquor traffic and endorse woman's suffrage. To become a member, one had to pay only a nominal membership fee and sign the pledge. Men could also join, but could not vote.

British Columbia's fledgling WCTU prospered, and by 1884 had 236 members in Victoria and 126 in Hope. Branches were soon extended to Burrard Inlet, Granville, Moodyville, Kamloops, Vernon, Revelstoke, Trail, Armstrong, Ladner and Sardis. In 1890 the group helped organize a Temperance and Moral Reform Association in Victoria to combat the twin evils of prostitution and drink. Other temperance groups were drawn in, including the Independent Order of Good Templars, Royal Templars of Temperance, and the Blue Ribbon Societies for the working class. Boycotts were organized against grocery stores that sold liquor, with attempts being made to ban liquor sales at fall fairs and other festive gatherings. But there was little of the wholesale vandalism of bars that occurred in the United States.

Brothels near the Pandora Avenue Methodist Church and St. Andrews Church in Victoria were roundly denounced, but supporters fought back. They openly hissed their disapproval in public meetings, scoffing that the houses had been there for years before the church was ever built, so should have "prior rights of location."[9] Although the Standard Theatre was shut down for lewdness, along with a few illegal saloons on Douglas and Pandora Street, British Columbia's temperance organizations accomplished little. In spite of the enthusiasm and large membership lists, meetings in Vancouver and Victoria rarely exceeded 60 people, and were often considerably less. In 1893, "The largest and most important women's meeting ever held in BC" numbered just seventy to eighty delegates.[10]

The greatest obstacle facing temperance groups was the almost complete lack of interest emanating from Victoria and Ottawa. Politicians ignored the prohibitionists or went out of their way to undermine them. Nowhere can this be better seen than in the massive railroad building projects of the 1880s and 1890s. The main line of the Canadian Pacific Railway (CPR) required thousands of transient workers to live in large construction camps like Donald, Yale and Vancouver. When temperance groups exerted pressure on the railways to go dry, the railways at first made concessions, and Ottawa passed the Public Works Peace Preservation Act, which granted the construction camps a 20-mile "dry" strip along the track. This was later increased to 40 miles.

The critical question, however, was who would enforce the law in connection with the railways, and this was left vague. In fact it was rarely enforced because of disputes over authority. The province licensed the saloons and hotels on the strips, but guarding the rail lines was a federal matter, left to the Dominion Police or the North West Mounted Police (NWMP). Dominion constables and the NWMP had worked together to protect the railhead in the prairie provinces, and it was assumed that they would do the same in British Columbia. Ottawa balked, however, and agreed to use the Dominion force to guard only actual construction sites and materials. Suppression of rowdiness, illicit drinking, gambling and prostitution in municipalities fell to the British Columbia Provincial Police (BCPP) along with a ragtag of local police. Life on the railhead was riotous. Gamblers and thugs lured the "navvies" (construction workers) into the bar, plied them with liquor, and robbed them. Drunken imbroglios over prostitutes and games of chance were common. Herbert Gowen, a Protestant churchman, gave this vivid description of payday at Yale during the 1880s:

> Yale bore at this time a most unenviable reputation. Payday was signalized by the most fearful riots, with which the all too slender

police force was powerless to contend. Drunkenness and disorder filled the place day and night. Fire kindled by lights held in hands unsteady with drink were of almost daily occurrence, the jail was overflowing and the justices weary. Tattered, dirt-bespattered drunkards rolled about the streets, wallowing in the mud, cursing and fighting, and driving all respectable people into the recesses of their homes, while saloon after saloon was added to the number already terribly in excess of the needs of the community.[11]

If the amount of drinking at Yale was representative, then clearly a coordinated police force would be needed to regulate drinking. Yet the rivalry between the various police forces spread only further confusion. In the narrow Fraser Canyon, the towns and construction sites overlapped, and it was hard to tell which was which. One was a federal responsibility, the other provincial. The stage was set for a confrontation. Matters reached a head in what came to be called the "constitutional war" of July 1885, at Farwell (now Revelstoke).

Whiskey-seller Jerry Hill arrived in town with eight cases of whiskey on his packhorse, and a legal provincial licence. The Dominion Police Commissioner George Johnson suddenly decided to enforce the little-used federal law banning alcohol in the construction zone, and arrested Hill. But John Kirkup, senior constable of the Provincial Police, saw the action as an affront to provincial jurisdiction. He demanded that Hill be released immediately and the whiskey returned. Johnson refused and warned Kirkup not to try anything rash, as he had appointed four NWMP constables and three special Dominion constables to guard the suspect. Two Provincial Policemen were dispatched to arrest the Dominion constable who had seized the whiskey, but they were suddenly arrested themselves and sentenced to two weeks in jail. The BCPP's Kirkup promptly jailed the Dominion Police Commissioner and his two special constables, charging them with assault.

Thus, within a few hours eight police constables were either in prison or facing serious charges. It appeared that bloodshed might result when the local magistrate, Malcolm Sproat (who naturally sided with the Provincial Police), described the situation as "a civil war" and darkly warned that "a squad of [federal] mounted police troopers . . . are immediately expected. . . . The future," he said, "may somewhat depend on the good sense of their officer . . ." and he refused to permit any obstruction of the law. Fortunately, cooler heads prevailed, everyone was finally released, and the affair was settled peacefully. Commissioner Johnson, who unwisely started the squabble in the first place, received a thirty dollar fine plus court costs for assault. As for Jerry Hill, he never did recover his whiskey; it vanished mysteriously while he was in the lock-up.[12]

It is apparent that the provincial authorities had more interest in settling scores with the federal police than in keeping liquor away from the railway workers. Alcohol not only brought in considerable tax revenues, it helped keep the workers happy. As an indication of the depth of their concern, Victoria appointed one lone provincial constable (out of over thirty-five available constables) to police the entire Fraser Canyon railroad line. He was the now familiar John Kirkup. In an emergency like the one at Farwell, the force could be augmented by "specials" temporarily deputized to assist, but this was discouraged because of cost. With thousands of single men blowing off steam in hundreds of brothels, bars and gambling dens, Kirkup's job was clearly impossible. The maximum fine under the Liquor Act for an unlicensed bar was only $150, which was easily covered by bootlegger profits within a few days.

Kirkup showed amazing fortitude under the circumstances. He did his best, breaking up brawls, closing down the more flagrant brothels and saloons, and jailing troublemakers. In one case, he apprehended a woman who had broken all the rules. In addition to her work as a madam, she was running a bar and gambling operation which sold to "mixed bloods." Before being taken off to jail she asked to change clothes, and suddenly presented herself to the constable in the nude. The stalwart Kirkup did not bat an eye. As he himself explained, "I wrapped a quilt around the struggling woman and carried her across town to the lockup."[13]

The federal Dominion Police, who really were supposed to be in charge, also kept a very low profile. After the "constitutional war," the two Dominion constables in the Fraser Canyon would patrol the construction zone and Canadian Pacific property only. They refused to have anything to do with policing the workers — even as a backup force. With such lax enforcement, bootleggers moved in to supply an ocean of beer and spirits. Drink arrived hidden in suitcases, pig carcasses, cans supposedly containing peaches and tin containers shaped like Bibles. Particularly favoured as a drink was "rock-cut," a potent local brew containing both alcohol and opium.

In September 1898, Ottawa again tried to address the contentious liquor issue. Prime Minister Wilfrid Laurier agreed to hold a country-wide Dominion Plebiscite in September 1898 which went far beyond the Local Option set out in the Scott Act. The issue would now be decided on a province-by-province basis by vote. The question on the ballot read: "Are you in favour of the passing of an Act prohibiting the manufacture, importation, or sale of spirits, wine, ale, beer, cider, and all other liquors for use as a beverage?" The newly elected Laurier had promised in his campaign speeches to put the question directly to the people, and had created the impression that he was at heart a prohibitionist. Soon after winning the election, however, he began to voice second thoughts about the idea — in particular the loss of millions of dollars in federal excise tax revenue. How would such a vast sum be replaced?

The Canada-wide Dominion Alliance for the Suppression of the Liquor Traffic launched a major campaign effort, printing nine million anti-drink leaflets, forty thousand cartoons and ten thousand posters, but the results of the plebiscite were frustrating and ambiguous. Although all of the provinces except Quebec were in favour of enacting prohibition, the vote was extremely close. With more than half a million votes cast, only a slim majority of 13,000, or 51.3 percent, voted in support of prohibition. Moreover, turnout was a disappointing 44 percent. Apathy ruled in British Columbia, which voted 5,731 to 4,756 in favour of prohibition — giving a plurality of less than one thousand.

Laurier was quick to sense the dangerous divisiveness of the issue, admitting that he was "in more dread of Temperance than of Senate reform."[14] Moreover, Quebec and other francophone communities were sharply at odds with the rest of Canada over religious and cultural issues, and this included prohibition. Using the low turnout and slender majority as an excuse, Laurier declared the Dominion plebiscite a failure. In this way, he washed his hands of a singularly divisive issue and turned the decision back to the provinces.

Yet this vote demonstrated that concern about liquor use in Canada registered as an important issue. If all adults had voted freely, prohibition would certainly have won, but at this time only white male British subjects over the age of twenty-one were eligible to cast their ballots. Women, who were among the most vocal in their anti-liquor feelings, were completely disenfranchised. Rural farmers, who also consistently voted dry, were hard at work in their fields bringing in the fall crop, and many did not vote. Understandably, the powerful temperance movement felt cheated. It had won at the polls, yet still lost the battle. Many drys blamed the defeat on the subversive influence of the Roman Catholic Church in Quebec, which opposed prohibition, or Ottawa's duplicity. They reluctantly moved their struggle to the provinces in hopes of a more sympathetic reception.

After the federal government abandoned the prohibitionists' cause in 1898, anti-liquor groups coalesced in Nova Scotia (1904), Prince Edward Island (1905), New Brunswick (1906), and Manitoba and Alberta (1907). They wished to impose even stricter laws, exercise the right to cut off liquor licences, and bring in a Local Option vote. In British Columbia, public opinion remained cool towards the Local Option and prohibition, in part because the provincial government took steps to curb the worst excesses of the bar. In spite of a run of nine undistinguished provincial premiers between 1882 and 1903, Victoria seemed willing to at least make a show of concern on the liquor issue. Problem drinkers were "siwashed" (a derogatory term for Natives commonly used during the early years of the province), or placed on an interdiction list that forbade them from purchasing alcohol. In 1887, a Habitual Drunkards Act allowed wives to petition to have their husband's property rights suspended and turned over to a court-appointed trustee if the husband were found to be a drunkard. The Act was rarely invoked. A Liquor Traffic Regulations Act was enacted in 1899, putting further pressure on drinking establishments. Gambling was forbidden in retail liquor outlets, and retail and wholesale licensing fees were raised to $200 per year, with an additional $500-bond to be posted. A provincial order-in-council appointed a two-person Board of Licence Commission for each district, with a one-year tenure. The Boards would only issue a liquor licence if two-thirds of the local licensed householders over the age of twenty-one signed a petition in favour. Chinese, Japanese and Natives were, of course, excluded.

The election of Richard McBride as premier in 1903 decisively tipped the balance further against the prohibitionists. The young, charismatic leader proved to be a brilliant politician who ran the province as a personal fiefdom for twelve years from 1903 to 1915. McBride was an exceedingly charming, witty and articulate man who never forgot a face. The premier personally enjoyed a sociable drink, and despised the Local Option movement, which he regarded, correctly, as a direct threat to his power base. With his trusted Attorney-General William (Billy) Bowser, the pair built a political machine of unprecedented power in the province. McBride was to prove a dedicated and unscrupulous enemy of prohibition until his early death in 1917.

By 1907 every other province in Canada, including Quebec, had the Local Option. The WCTU and its allies argued that the province of British Columbia had to elevate her moral standards and join with the rest of the country. A Local Option League led by Vancouver businessman E.B. Morgan soon had fifty branches in the province. Although the movement excited little interest at first, a well-staged convention held in Vancouver late in 1908 drew delegates from around the province. Considerable pains were taken to avoid any sort of divisive religious affiliation. Anyone could join, regardless of race, creed or political orientation. In addition to the Local Option, the League wanted the right to elect licensed commissioners, and to recall those who failed to reflect the true views of the community.

By the end of 1909, more than seventy branches had been established, and petitions in favour of a Local Option law had collected the signatures of 10,000 voters (male) and 25,000 non-voters (women, Asians, Natives, etc.) in the province.[15] But the League's demands ran afoul of the liquor patronage machine in Victoria. The legislature had earlier passed an order-in-council which ensured that only locally appointed officials could issue licences for drinking establishments. This may sound like local control, but in practice the idea actually encouraged corruption and cronyism. Local bosses with political connections rapidly took up the reins. Bribes and kickbacks determined who would become commissioner, not the interests of the district as a whole. McBride was clearly loath to surrender control over the lucrative trade in alcohol.

The premier procrastinated on holding a Local Option plebiscite, then grudgingly agreed to combine it with a provincial election in November 1909. With great cunning, however, the government refused to release the exact wording of the plebiscite until just days before the election, and deliberately sought to confuse the electorate about whether the plebiscite was an actual vote for the Local Option, or merely a vote for the idea of having a Local Option. McBride's Conservative party focused instead on the great railroad projects. On the subject of alcohol, confusion and apathy ruled.

Not surprisingly, the plebiscite results were badly flawed by "voting irregularities." Not enough ballots had been printed, and many were mysteriously misplaced. Scrutineers were not allowed to oversee the vote in some districts, and one out of twenty ballots was disqualified for minor irregularities. The government kept no permanent record of the plebiscite, and the results were never officially tabulated or printed. It was evident that the McBride regime had no intention of accepting a Local Option law. But these irregularities were conveniently ignored in the wake of the Conservatives' tumultuous victory celebrations. McBride's Party of Prosperity swept the house with a thirty-four-seat majority — leaving only two Liberals and two Socialists to form the opposition. Unofficial sources claimed that 22,779 voted for the local option, with 19,084 against, but many voted for neither, leaving the total slightly less then the required 50 percent of BC's voters who cast their ballots for a candidate. The plebiscite created a paradoxical situation in which the Local Option vote won in numbers, but still fell short. It quietly went down to defeat, drowned out by the joyous news of the booming railroad bubble.[16]

To defuse discontent over the irregularities of the vote, McBride was willing to make further concessions to the drys. Saloonkeepers were required to keep their establishments clean, both morally and physically, and they needed a character reference signed by the Chief of Police to ply their trade. Sunday closing laws were tightened up, and in 1911 changes to the Liquor Act allowed municipalities to close down all saloons if they so chose. Two years later a provincial law was passed which required hotels to offer at least thirty rooms to their clientele. The city of Vancouver was even more demanding: hotels had to provide 100 rooms and a fully equipped dining room. All of these renovations involved considerable expense for hotel and bar owners.[17]

After 1910, Attorney-General Billy Bowser consolidated provincial liquor powers further by ending the practice of allowing local boards to license saloons in unincorporated areas. Instead, this power was placed in the hands of the police, who were directly responsible to the Attorney-General's office. Local constables ensured that saloonkeepers made their mandatory political contributions to the Conservative party, and promoted the right candidate to their customers. Any barkeep who failed to deliver the votes, or supported the wrong candidate, lost his licence. In fact, the relation between saloon owners and the police was highly symbiotic. When things became too rowdy, the beleaguered owner was forced to call upon the police for protection — and pay for it.

The web of patronage seemed to stretch everywhere. Public works projects such as road and bridge building needed workers, but anyone hoping for a job had to show the correct political loyalties. In Victoria and Vancouver, the powerful police commission ran the liquor licence business. It consisted of a political appointee, the mayor, and an alderman of his choice. Conservative mayors, bank managers, timber magnates and mining barons joined the pro-business Beaver Club to promote their agendas. By 1911 there were seventeen branches across the provinces advising the Tory patronage machine.[18]

In desperation, the Local Option League staged a convention and asked that a vote should at least be permitted in the areas that had voted for it in 1909, but this reasonable request was ignored. The movement began to lose momentum, and the issue was no longer considered relevant to provincial politics. The tiny band of Liberals in Victoria who had made the liquor issue and women's suffrage a central part of their platform took another brutal drubbing in the 1912 provincial elections. The Liberals were annihilated from the House, and only two Socialists from the coalfields of Vancouver Island remained to face the Tories.

By 1912, McBride seemed unstoppable and, with his massive majority in the House, could do as he pleased. Times were good, and the province was prospering. The worst excesses of the bar had been tamed, and even the moderate Local Option movement had faded from view. Some other event or social pressure would be needed to tip the scales decisively in the public mind in favour of banning liquor. That would come soon enough with the First World War.

CHAPTER 4

THE WAR, FOOD AND BOOZE

AS IT TURNED OUT, McBride's Party of Prosperity was resting on shaky foundations. A severe economic downturn followed the election in 1912, which ripped away the facade of economic complacency and severely weakened the Premier's hold on the province. World commodity prices fell, depressing prices for metals, fish, timber and agricultural products. Foreign investors withdrew credit as war clouds gathered. Unemployment skyrocketed, and suddenly "there was everything to sell and no one to buy." McBride's policy of boosting prosperity by selling off Crown forests and agricultural land at fire-sale prices could only last so long. By 1912, over 11 million acres (around 80 percent) of the best timberland had been alienated from the Crown, and 90 percent of the province's scarce agricultural land had been sold to speculators.[1] As a result, government revenues plummeted. Bitter labour unrest among railroad workers and miners led to shortages and strikes. The great Vancouver Island Coal Strike of 1912 to 1914 saw the most violent worker rebellion in the province's history, with thousands walking off the job to protest dangerous working conditions, the failure of the coal companies to recognize their new union (The United Mine Workers of America) and other issues. There were riots between scabs and miners. Bombs were thrown, shots exchanged and houses torched. At first Billy Bowser tried to stem the violence with tough Provincial Police specials nicknamed "Bowser's Bulldogs." But when they arrived by ferry in Nanaimo, a riot broke out; an angry mob shot a constable and stoned the chief of police. Twelve hundred soldiers were ordered in, and hundreds of protestors were arrested, including several young boys. The American anarchist Mother Jones received standing ovations on the Island and mainland when she declared, "If the capitalists rob us to buy guns for their hired assassins we will have to buy guns ourselves."[2] In addition, racial tension between Asians and whites worsened with the economic downturn. McBride and Bowser's decision to import hundreds of cheap Chinese workers to break the coal strikes further infuriated the miners.

Scandal dogged the administration and further discredited the McBride regime. The giant Dominion Trust Company defaulted, costing some five thousand shareholders their savings and throwing Vancouver into financial chaos. It was discovered that large, unauthorized loans had been made to the company's directors, who had close ties to the government. But the greatest disaster of all was the sudden crash of the premier's grandly ambitious railway schemes, which had formed the core of his development plan for the province. A bewildering array of competing lines had been planned for the province: the Grand Trunk Pacific, Canadian Northern Pacific, Kettle River Valley, Kootenay Central, and the Esquimalt & Nanaimo. Now, the schemes were collapsing and the government faced a debt of tens of millions of dollars. The railroad loans and bond guarantees, so casually granted by McBride earlier, returned now to haunt the province with a vengeance.

The sudden outbreak of the First World War in August 1914 threw yet another spanner into the workings of the provincial economy. In the early days, there was a great outpouring of enthusiasm and patriotism as young men, fearful that the war would be over by Christmas, rushed off to enlist. The huge labour force on which the economy depended decamped overnight into the training fields and trenches, turning the province's urban areas into ghost towns. Land prices stagnated and then fell, while wartime demand stimulated inflation. The provincial surpluses from the sale of government lands could not be sustained, and the collapse of the railroad bubble wreaked further havoc on the provincial economy. By 1914, provincial liability for one railroad — the Great Northern Pacific — had reached over $33 million, and indirect liability totalled over $80 million.

Anyone leafing through the newspapers of the time cannot help being shocked by the change of tone after August 1914. Words rarely heard before dominated the news: trenches, chlorine gas, U-boats, aeroplanes, tanks, Zeppelins, dumdum bullets, Moaning Minnies, machine-guns, snipers and flamethrowers. Much was made of the superiority of the Canadian foot soldier, who, it was said, never surrendered. Every action was declared a Canadian victory. There were countless photos of stern young faces bravely marching off to fight the despotic "Hun," followed in the back pages by grim columns listing the dead, maimed and missing. By 1916, the war had degenerated into a grisly game of attrition as first one side, and then the other, threw itself at heavily defended trench fortifications bristling with machine guns and heavy artillery. Ypres, the Somme, Vimy Ridge, Passchendaele, Mons, and other battles followed in dreary succession. A slow grinding down of the enemy became the goal, and the cost was horrific.

It has been estimated that fewer than half of the bodies on all sides were ever recovered from the battlefields. In total 619,636 Canadians joined the Canadian Expeditionary Force; 59,544 were killed and an incredible 172,950 were injured. British Columbia did her part by shipping off 55,750 troops, with 43,000 going to

France, Belgium and England. By the November armistice in 1918, 6,255 soldiers from British Columbia had perished, and more than 13,600 — almost one-quarter of those who served overseas — were wounded.[3]

At home, the popular fascination with wealth, speculation and greed faded as British Columbians became obsessed with the war. Improving society now meant making it more functional and better capable of defeating the hated enemy. People became more socially conservative. A decrease in ostentation was accompanied by a surge in church attendance. The questions of women's suffrage, prohibition and workers' rights were re-examined in light of the new patriotism. Perhaps these noble causes had a role to play in winning the war, as well as improving society. Every sacrifice was expected if it would bring victory and release from the terrible conflict.

Indeed, as soon as Canada entered the war, the old moral arguments against alcohol, which had failed to carry the day in 1909, were now strongly augmented by a new imperative — the overwhelming importance of food in the war effort. Everyone agreed that providing nutrition for soldiers and civilians should be a central part of Canada's contribution to the Allied effort. And it just so happened that the production of alcoholic beverages consumed large quantities of both sugar and grain.

In the early days of the war, the federal government unanimously passed the War Measures Act, granting itself near-dictatorial powers over individual civil rights and the economy. These powers included the right to detain and deport enemy aliens, the right of censorship to control communication and transportation, the right to appropriate and dispose of property, and the right of central planners to control manufacturing, trading, farming and food production. As the war dragged on, Canada took on the task of feeding millions of Allied soldiers, prisoners of war, refugees, and the beleaguered civilian population in Europe. The food burden dramatically increased, and the situation was seen as so serious in Ottawa that a Food Controller, W.J. Hanna, was appointed in June

1917 to coordinate production throughout the country. Crop land was dramatically expanded, prices fixed, and a system of permits and licences instituted to regulate the market. Despite droughts, early frosts, storms and an epidemic of wheat rust, the value of food exports jumped to astonishing levels. Production revenues shot up from $137,011,030 in 1914 to $710,619,400 in 1918.[4]

This huge expansion in overseas food exports naturally created shortages at home, which led the Food Controller to issue dire warnings. Unless the country made a commitment to use food economically, Canadians would face "starvation" during the winter of 1917. Hanna further noted that if it were to be a question of hunger at home or hunger at the front, the boys in the trenches would not be allowed to suffer.[5] While these threats seem a little far-fetched today, they offer clear evidence of Ottawa's concern and determination. The food measures were harsh and far-reaching. In public eating places, beef and bacon were prohibited on Tuesdays and Fridays and could appear no more than once a day during the rest of the week. In addition, substitutes like potatoes, cornbread and oatcakes had to be offered at every meal where white bread was served. "French pastry, iced cakes, or biscuits or cake with icing or cane sugar between the layers or added to the exterior . . ." were also forbidden. The government's particular abhorrence of hoarding was noted in the Canada Food Board pamphlets:

> The food hoarders are working against the common good and even against the very safety of the country. Hoarding food in households is unnecessary and selfish. The government is protecting the food supply and its people.
> *Loyalty in little things is the foundation of national strength. Disloyalty in little things gives aid to the enemy. Keep the pledge.*[6]

Penalties for violators were stiff, with fines running from $100 to $1,000 and/or up to three months in jail. In the war situation, squandering precious food commodities on alcohol was simply unacceptable. The use of wheat for brewing and distilling was strictly prohibited, except for the production of military munitions, and even in that case a licence had to be obtained from the Food Controller. A summary conviction brought a penalty of up to $5,000 — several years' wages for the average working man. There were few convictions, as almost everyone accepted the restrictions as part of their patriotic duty. Commercial breweries continued to produce beer, but at a reduced level.

The food issue gave new life to the prohibition movement in the province and, by 1915, organizations began exerting aggressive pressure on Premier McBride to reconsider prohibition. Businessmen from Vancouver, Victoria, Chilliwack and other urban areas met and planned their strategy. A prohibition dinner at Dominion Hall in Vancouver drew more than 500 people, and was concluded when all raised their glasses in a non-alcoholic toast to the cause. John Nelson, an avid prohibitionist who became editor and owner of the Vancouver *World* in May 1915, turned his paper into a one-issue soapbox for prohibition. In a front-page editorial, he called for drinkers and non-drinkers alike to put aside their differences and unite to form a common front for the war effort. He argued that the war campaign on the home front was an economic one, and that total abstainers would find themselves "reinforced by the votes of club men and moderate and even immoderate drinkers throughout the province." The candid opinion of "sensible men," he added, was that no country on a war-footing had "any business permitting the continuance of a trade which imposes unnecessary burdens on industry and commerce and entails worse ravages than war itself."[7]

The crowds at rallies increased, and finally a large convention with temperance speakers Nellie McClung and Principal Lloyd was set for August 25 and 26, 1915, at Hamilton Hall in Vancouver. A Mr. W.C. Findlay, of whom more will be heard later, oversaw a staff of seventy-five ushers to seat the audience. Speaking before an estimated crowd of four thousand, Lloyd proclaimed: "There is only one liberty in this world, and that is the liberty to do right. Other liberty is simply licence." Nellie McClung, promoted as "Canada's greatest entertainer and oratoress," had long been passionately involved in social reform and women's rights. As usual, McClung got right to the heart of the matter:

> We women have had nothing to do with the liquor business except to pay the price. . . . [We] get none of the pleasure of drinking, which the men are supposed to get, and the money which is made, also goes to the men, but the long price, the price in sorrow and suffering, that is paid by the woman at home.[8]

And then driving home the point that women must become involved in the war effort, she compared women's struggle against alcohol to Belgium's attempt to free itself from Germany's brutal occupation.

Women, in particular, were attracted to the wartime prohibition movement, seeing it as a way that they could make a contribution to the war effort. They now worked in the factories, planted the crops and managed the households while their men were off in the trenches. Along with these jobs came wages and financial independence, which reaffirmed their growing desire for greater participation in politics and society. The majority were light drinkers or teetotallers, and the old alliance between the supporters of women's suffrage and prohibition remained strong. It was apparent to all that, if a vote were called on these two issues, British Columbia's women would work strongly for the passage of both.

McBride was deluged with letters and petitions and, the day before the August convention, grandly announced a new plebiscite on alcohol. But the premier really had promised all and granted nothing in his announcement. He revealed neither the date, nor what was to be decided, nor even what the vote signified. Such vague assurances inflamed the prohibitionists, who well remembered the premier's similar litany of deceptions during the 1909 Local Option struggle.

Following up on the successful Vancouver convention, a People's Prohibition Movement was organized, which quickly became the nemesis of wet forces in the province. Regular meetings were scheduled, and a group of prominent activists was elected to staff the organization. A short time later in April 1917, the People's Prohibition Movement renamed itself the People's Prohibition Association (PPA). (For the sake of simplicity, the more familiar PPA will be employed throughout.) Powerful businessmen such as Jonathan Rogers of the Vancouver Board of Trade, John Nelson of the *World,* E. B Morgan, President of North-West Trust, George F. Gibson and George J. Hammond joined the organization. At first, no membership dues were paid and no charters signed, which effectively kept power out of the hands of the rank and file. Later there was a nominal fee of a dollar, which included a three-month subscription to the *World.*

The early minutes of the PPA were filled with bitter animus over McBride's tedious foot-dragging. The organization announced that it "deeply regrets that the Premier Sir Richard McBride in his final reply has failed to grant the requests of the People's Prohibition Association in principles which it deems vital." Members stressed the group's non-partisan nature by "standing on record for the principle of prohibition in preference to any political party."[9]

The premier sought escape from his travails by travelling to England, but his disappearance from the local scene accomplished nothing. After three months of socializing and many rounds of parties, McBride returned home to find his popularity at a record low. At first he seemed oblivious to the rising clamour over women's suffrage and prohibition, but soon the growing resentment caused by the failing economy, scandals, debts, and the nagging issues of women's suffrage and prohibition proved too much to overcome. In November 1915, McBride capitulated. He sent a letter to the PPA, grudgingly allowing a vote on both suffrage and prohibition in the next provincial election. But he decided not to stay in British Columbia for the results; in mid-December, at age forty-five, the premier announced his resignation, and accepted the post of British Columbia's Agent-General in London.

Many were mystified when Richard McBride stepped down willingly, curious as to why he would accept such a lowly position as Agent-General. Was he angling for something better in England, or did he just wish to escape his humiliating loss of popularity at home? Whatever the case, McBride never again played a major role in British Columbia politics. As will been seen, however, he was not yet finished with the prohibition movement.

As McBride's fortunes sank, Bowser's ascended. Billy Bowser, master of political intrigue and backroom deals, was first elected to a Vancouver riding in 1907. After he became Attorney-General early in McBride's tenure, the tendrils of his power began to reach into the police, the liquor trade and the Victoria patronage machine. Amoral, pugnacious, and blunt to a fault, he claimed to know how things really worked in politics. He boasted, "I am a man of the world and I know from other transactions, not only with Indians, but other people, that a bit of greasing sometimes has to be done."[10] In spite of his considerable political skills, Bowser did not at first understand the depth of reformist sentiment in the province.

The Little Kaiser, as he came to be called, ignored the numerous letters, resolutions, delegations and committees that daily deluged the premier's office from the People's Prohibition Association. It was only after three critical by-elections were held in Vancouver, Rossland and Victoria in the early spring of 1916 that Bowser began to understand the seriousness of the situation. All of the old scandals were being hauled out and rehashed — the railroads, the shady sales of crown land and timber, the backroom wheeling and dealing, the financial cronyism, and so on. The opposition Liberals made the demand for popular referenda on suffrage and prohibition their central campaign issue and, for the first time in many years, they inflicted a serious defeat on the Conservatives. Two important Tory cabinet ministers lost their seats to the Liberals by large majorities, and the third kept his seat by only twelve votes. One of the winners was Harlan Carey Brewster, who would soon become the new Liberal leader.

Bowser at first blamed the losses on meddling by the People's Prohibition Association, but changed his mind after seeing the tallies. Like McBride before him, he attempted to disarm his prohibitionist opponents with half measures. Bars, saloons and clubs would face further restrictions on hours of operation. Such measures were not enough, and continued pressure from the PPA finally led him to announce in early March, before a large prohibition delegation, that the government would now go further. Instead of offering a mere plebiscite, Bowser suggested binding referenda on both suffrage and prohibition, these to be held during the next provincial election. A plebiscite on prohibition would involve a direct vote, but it would be a statement of opinion by the public, which had no legal effect. A referendum, on the other hand, would have more weight because the results would be legally binding. The crowd rose and gave the Little Kaiser three hearty cheers. When queried as to why it had taken him so many months to come up with a coherent policy, he conveniently blamed ill health. The referenda on suffrage and prohibition were set to coincide with the provincial election set for the fall of 1916.

The PPA was ecstatic, expressing "deep satisfaction" with Bowser and warmly commending "his frank promise that his government would prepare without delay a measure satisfactory to the People's Prohibition Association to come into effect on January 1, 1917."[11] In spite of this notable victory, some doubted Bowser's sincerity. The Liberal leader, Harlan Brewster, complained with some justification that the premier was stealing his party's main plank, since the Liberals had fought against John Barleycorn since 1912. He could, of course, do nothing less than support the Conservative referenda, but he may have guessed that Bowser was up to something, since he offered to introduce his own Act if Bowser's failed to pass. Still, with the two referenda promised, prohibitionists, lawyers, and members of the legislature immediately began work on drawing up a formal Prohibition Act to be put before the people.

The situation in the province was complex, with many competing interests. Most people would appear to have had mixed feelings about the vote. Many liked an occasional drink, but there was also a strong sense that something needed to be done on the home front to help win the war. The politicians sensed this ambivalence.

Even though both McBride and Bowser had been willing to support some sort of ballot on prohibition, they remained cautious when it came to committing themselves to one side or the other. The campaign soon degenerated into a raucous shouting match on the fringes, with the extremists dominating the debate.

The PPA hierarchy was made up of hard-line Methodists and Presbyterians, who led a devoted army of churchmen, women, teenagers and other "decent patriots." The drys genuinely believed that the war could not be won without prohibition, and wanted the abolition of liquor enshrined in law as soon as possible. The staunchest opposition from the wets was directed by the Merchants' Protective Association (MPA), who had business interests at stake. Labour groups like The Vancouver Trades and Labour Council and the Workers' Equal Rights Association were also prominent. The MPA had its own stable of high-profile merchants and lawyers, such as H.V. Pratt of the Hudson's Bay Company, J.W. Ambery, manager of Hiram Walker & Company, A. Edward Tulk, a prominent lawyer, and Nels Nelson, owner of New Westminster Breweries.

Unlike the People's Prohibition Association, the MPA held few rallies, preferring to concentrate on written advertisements, leaflets and combative editorials. Hard liquor was ignored while the healthful benefits of beer were highly praised. There was a scramble to buy up small town newspapers and convert them to the cause. A. Edward Tulk and a Captain Worsnop, manager of the Leland Hotel in Kamloops, unsuccessfully tried to take over the *Kamloops Telegram* that summer, but were stopped by the PPA.[12] With the exception of the *World*, most newspapers in the province had ties to labour and business so they tended to be affiliated with the wets. Debate grew so heated that some papers sold space in the editorial pages at classified advertisement rates. The MPA was quick to lament the dearth of honest discussion by politicians in Victoria:

> A very peculiar feature in connection with the consideration of the British Columbia Prohibition Act by the Provincial Legislature is that during the many times that it was before the House for discus-

sion, not a single word was uttered by any member of the Legislature in praise of the Act, or in defence of the principles enunciated by the measure.

The MPA noted also that people of all political stripes were reluctant to use the term "Prohibition Act." Nor were they willing to outline in "what way the legislation would be for the best interests of the Province."[13]

As it turned out, many wanted to delay the vote until after the war, when life would return to normal. A petition of some 34,000 names was submitted by the Merchants' Protective Association, asking that no vote on liquor be held until after the war's conclusion. The MPA also urged that, if prohibition went ahead, full compensation be paid to hotel owners and brewers. Others complained that the very freedoms they were fighting for in Europe were about to be crushed in Canada by war hysteria. The British Columbia Provincial Secretary received the following note from a soldier. It was accompanied by a news clipping describing a riot involving soldiers and participants in a temperance gathering in Toronto:

> If a vote must be taken please insist that it be done 6 months after peace is declared by which time we can all be home again.
> Yours Faithfully, WESTERN SCOTT

This "Western Scott" protested that the soldiers did not want rioting in British Columbia of the sort that Toronto had seen, but that the soldiers were fighting overseas for the liberty of all people, including the "puritans" who wanted to take away essential freedoms.[14]

The workingman remained strongly wet. There was an estimated 3,500 people, with at least 6,000 dependents, directly employed in the saloon and brewing industry. The sudden closing down of all of the breweries, bars, saloons, and liquor outlets would impose tremendous hardship on those workers. But it must be said that hostility to prohibition was not universal in the Labour movement. Some argued that liquor actually defeated the workingman by distracting his mind and keeping him complacently ignorant. In 1916, the *BC Federationist* noted that a sober worker "is far more apt to be a thinking one and such men are dangerous. He who formerly spent some of his wages for booze, might in case of the victory of prohibition, turn . . . to the purchase of socialist literature for instance, and then the employers' interest would be threatened by a far greater danger than ever lurked behind a liquor befuddled brain."[15] Nevertheless, with so many jobs at stake, organized labour had to vote a resounding "no" on prohibition. For them, employment, not booze, was the central issue:

> Life and death to the working class is not a question of beer or no beer. It is first, last and always, under present industrial conditions, a question of jobs. If prohibition became law tomorrow in Vancouver, New Westminster and Victoria, would that fact increase the number of jobs available for the unemployed who now abound in each of those cities? We do not believe it would.[16]

Workers pointed to other reasons for keeping beer legal. Malted beverages were described as absolutely "essential" for the physical and mental well being of the Canadian workingman. Unlike spirits, beer was the drink of moderation. It was not an intoxicant; it was food. A delegation of mine workers from Cumberland presented a six-thousand-signature petition to the House, endorsed by the Labour Councils of Victoria and Vancouver. Joe Naylor, representing the union local, noted,

> . . . the men required to labour for the most part underground endured strain of the most arduous nature, and it had been found that the solid properties of beer to a large extent counterbalanced the loss of energy from the physical tax endured.

Naylor contended that the heavy wartime demand was both "arduous and strenuous," with a "great physical tax on the system." The use of beer, he found, "is as great a necessity to us as solid food." It apparently also kept the worker healthy and productive. Citing the supposed physical inferiority of the Asiatic races to whom beer and whiskey were "as strangers," Naylor declared that "the average robustness of the British Columbia miner was partly due to reasonable use of beer as a stimulant." He also warned ominously that "further Industrial strife" would result if prohibition were forced on the working man.[17]

Organized labour also questioned the hysterical, intolerant tone of the prohibitionists. There was always the dark suspicion that they wanted more than just the simple eradication of alcohol. Perhaps the real aim was absolute social control and the destruction of democracy? In "Prohibition and Freedom of the Individual," Dr. J. Emerson Roberts delivered a passionate warning regarding the authoritarian dangers of prohibition enforced by the state:

> There is only one transcendent question: It is whether we shall confer upon the state the authority to invade our private lives, to cross the threshold of our homes, and there, by force and coercion, dictate and control our conduct.

What was at stake, Roberts argued, was the freedom of the individual in the face of an attack by forces "garbed in the vestments of religion and professing its love for mankind," who wanted to destroy liberty, "the one thing for which the race has struggled longest and suffered the most."[18]

For their part, the PPA organizers recognized that the workingman had little interest in instituting prohibition. One member estimated at a planning meeting that unless major efforts were made to reach the workers, prohibition would only pull in 10 percent of the labour vote. As a result, the prohibitionists went out of their way to portray themselves as the true friends of labour in their pamphlets. In *Labor and Liquor: An Appeal to the Intelligence and Legitimate Self-Interest of the Workers of B.C.*, W. D. Bayley was careful to use the inclusive "our" and "we":

> Men of the Labor Movement. . . . Let us first warn you of the "double-cross" stunt. The liquor interests are parading as the friends of Labor as against Capital. When as a matter of fact the liquor trade is the meanest branch of Capitalism we have. Averaging it all around this trade employs one-quarter the number of men, pays one-

quarter the amount of wages and uses one-quarter the amount of raw material as the general average of capital invested in such businesses as clothing, shoes, lumber etc. It outdistances many times over, all the ordinary lines of capitalistic enterprises in the percentage of profit reaped.[19]

These transparent attempts to win over the working man usually fell on deaf ears.

In these early skirmishes both wets and drys seemed fairly evenly matched. The vote would be close. Many observers felt that prohibition would founder along the coast, the result of the strong labour vote, but would do well in the Fraser Valley and the rural "Bible Belt" interior of the province. It was now time to take the issues of suffrage and prohibition to the people.

CHAPTER 5

THE PURITY ELECTION OF 1916
"The Tighter the Law, the Fewer Get Tight"

THE BRITISH COLUMBIA Prohibition Act went before the legislature on May 23, 1916. It was speedily passed on May 31, along with an Act to allow both the prohibition and suffrage referenda to take place during the 1916 provincial election. Every elector would receive three ballot-papers, each of a different colour: one for the election, one for the vote on suffrage and the last for prohibition. The two questions were plainly stated: "Are you in favour of the Extension of the Electoral Franchise to Women? Yes or No. Are you in favour of bringing the 'British Columbia Prohibition Act' into Force? Yes or No." If passed by a majority of the province's electorate, women's suffrage would come into force on March 1, 1917; prohibition would follow on July 1. Bowser set the date of September 14, 1916, for the provincial election and the dual referenda.

The Prohibition Act was twenty pages long, hastily written,

complex, and obsessively bureaucratic. To be sure, one could still legally make and drink liquor, but one could drink only in one's private "dwelling house." The question remained: what constituted a dwelling house? Not just any old house would do. According to the law, a dwelling was

> a separate dwelling with a separate door or ingress and egress and actually and exclusively occupied and used as a private residence.... 'A private dwelling house' shall include also a suite of rooms in an apartment block, in a city, separated and closed off by walls from all other rooms in such block, and without any door or opening whereby communication may be had with any other room save doors opening into a main or common hall leading, with or without stairs, into a street or lane, and in which suite there are facilities for cooking and a family actually residing, cooking, sleeping and taking their meals.[1]

An office, workshop, warehouse, club room, public hall, shop, place of business, hotel, boarding house or apartment leased to someone other than those drinking was not a legal dwelling under the proposed law. Possession of alcohol anywhere other than one's private dwelling would be punishable by a fine of $50 to $100, or thirty-five to sixty days in jail.

At this time, a mild 2.5 proof "near-beer" (1.25 percent alcohol) would be permitted in hotels and unlicensed "jitney" bars, named after the many automobiles carrying paying passengers that were now on the streets in the province. Being about one-fifth as strong as the normal brew, near-beer was not considered an alcoholic beverage. Some British Columbia brewers finessed an even weaker concoction of 1 percent called "beerless," which came to be treated as little more than a soft drink. There were no restrictions of any sort on the sale of these weak brews, which soon caused problems, particularly among the young drinkers.

The law was extremely hard on those who sold, bartered or gave alcoholic beverages to anyone. A first offence brought a mandatory six- to twelve-months hard labour in the provincial prison, with no option of a fine; a second offence would send one off to

▲ Newspaper cartoon, 1912–13, depicting Nellie McClung and the WCTU (the Woman's Christian Temperance Union) as the sun eclipsing the figure of Intemperance with his drinking and smoking. Youth watches as the eclipse becomes Tee-total. (COURTESY BC ARCHIVES, 85186)

▲ The stern-faced ladies of Nanaimo's WCTU in 1904.
(COURTESY CITY OF NANAIMO ARCHIVES, J3-92)

▲ Temperance House, built 1876 on the northeast corner
of Bastion and Skinner Streets, Nanaimo, BC.
(COURTESY CITY OF NANAIMO ARCHIVES, C3-4)

▲ Marrah's Liquor Store in Nanaimo happily served both the occupying Army and strikers during the Great Vancouver Island Coal Strike of 1913–14. (COURTESY CITY OF NANAIMO ARCHIVES, C3-40)

▲ The Lansdowne Brewery in Nanaimo produced excellent beer from 1886 until prohibition ended production in 1918.
(COURTESY CITY OF NANAIMO ARCHIVES, C3-114)

▲ The Union Brewery on Wallace Street, Nanaimo. One of booze magnate Henry Reifel's many liquor concerns, it failed to survive prohibition and was closed in 1919.
(COURTESY CITY OF NANAIMO ARCHIVES, C3-46)

▲ Delivering barrels of beer with the Union Brewery Company's team. Some breweries continued to use horses even after the jitney car invasion. (COURTESY CITY OF NANAIMO ARCHIVES, Q1-40)

▲ Urban liquor stores like this one in downtown Victoria offered a bewildering variety of alcoholic refreshments before prohibition, c. 1910. (COURTESY CITY OF VICTORIA ARCHIVES, PD80-6895 MO6514)

▲ The well-stocked shelves of the Bodena Hotel Bar, Nelson, BC, c. 1898.
(COURTESY BC ARCHIVES, B-03151)

▲ A well-heeled saloon at the corner of Broad and Johnson Streets, Victoria, BC, c. 1914. (COURTESY BC ARCHIVES, F-02562)

▶ Bars in the late 19th century were often ornate affairs, selling many varieties of liquor and, as the sign indicates, even fresh milk. The Manhattan Saloon, Nelson, 1896. (COURTESY BC ARCHIVES, B-03135)

jail for twelve to twenty-one months. Police could raid and break into any home, business, or vehicle without a warrant if they believed that liquor was being improperly kept or sold. The presence of illicit liquor within one's premises could be considered presumptive proof of sale, and guilt would be ascribed to the legal occupant — even if a servant, employee or some other person had committed the offence. Furthermore, once on trial, the accused would have to prove his innocence, rather then having the Crown prove guilt as in all other criminal trials.

There were a few exceptions to these draconian regulations, and they actually infuriated many by appearing to cater to the rich and privileged. There still remained two easy ways to obtain alcohol: liquor could still be legally imported from outside the province to one's dwelling place; and doctors and veterinarians could prescribe it as a remedy for sick patients. Since both of these solutions required money, opponents dismissed the Act as "rank, miserable, class legislation." An advertisement in the *Nanaimo Free Press* declared, "The prohibition act is a rich man's law. . . . The act is directly aimed at the man of moderate means. . . . Such provisions are class legislation of a pronounced type. Read the Act Vote No."[2]

The ugly class overtones of the bill were a major weakness, and they rapidly became the focus of much complaint and resentment. Of course, ministers of the gospel were also given an exemption to possess wine for sacramental purposes though not as a beverage. But good beer by the glass, the workingman's standard, would be strictly forbidden. Many scratched their head about the absurdities of the law. How much sense did it make to declare illegal British Columbia beer brewed locally and cheaply, when the same beer could be legally ordered from Calgary, but only at great expense? Some wags argued that allowing the affluent to import liquor by the gallon would actually increase debauchery and drunkenness, whereas the stolid worker with his occasional glass of beer was an exemplar of moderation.

As campaign material, both the Merchants' Protective Association and the People's Prohibition Association published pamphlets containing the lengthy text of the prohibition law, along with scathing commentary. *Prohibition Act? The Truth* ridiculed the harsh prison sentences for distributing alcohol:

> This is another section of the Act which indicates fanaticism, that is, the unlimited extent to which a person intoxicated with a hobby will press his insane conclusions. It defeats its own object. Imagine a Statute that permits a person to legally give his friend a glass of beer in his home but if he gives his aged father a glass of beer on a fishing trip, he is guilty of such a heinous crime that, without the option of a fine he must be imprisoned with hard labour for a period not less than six months. The Magistrate hearing the case has no alternative.
>
> Can a sane man believe that such a provision will be enforced? Why, therefore, pass Statutes knowing they can never be carried out? What right thinking man would assist in a conviction with such results?[3]

The prohibitionists countered with *The Real Truth About the Prohibition Act*:

> They imagine that the police forces and all prohibitionists will at once embark on a campaign of espionage and blackmail. If we should lose at the polls it will be solely owing to the fact that our good citizens and church people read [A.E.] Tulk's advertisements and not the Act itself. Our next campaign will be for Federal Dominion-wide Prohibition.[4]

The question of compensation for business losses remained troubling, since it was recognized that bars and breweries had spent large sums in building up their businesses. The total value of the industry ran to between $5 million and $20 million, depending on who was doing the accounting. The brewing industry had invested heavily in hotels during the prosperous McBride years, and now it appeared that both breweries and hotel bars were about to be legislated out of existence. Many felt that denying compensation was not only unfair but also "un-British." Confiscation of private property by government without some return was frowned upon under

English Common Law. Should not the same rules apply in British Columbia? Hotel owners complained that they had been deliberately misled, and forced to waste money on useless improvements.

The PPA responded with a brief to the provincial secretary, complaining that the merchants were willing tools of the liquor lobby, trying to confuse the voters and conduct a "successful raid upon the treasury." Who would get compensation, and for what, they asked. The hotel properties would still be perfectly usable, mortgages would remain intact, and excess stocks of alcohol could be sold out of province. Let the liquor barons turn to denatured alcohol, extracts, vinegar and soft drinks to make up for lost sales. A liquor licence was not real property; it was a piece of paper that allowed the sale of liquor. How could there be any compensation when there was no loss of property? Moreover, no other state or province that enacted prohibition had ever offered compensation to saloon or hotel owners. The PPA made it clear why they did not want to pay the liquor barons a penny in a 1916 pamphlet titled *Shall We Compensate the Liquor-Man?*:

> The common-sense justice of the community would never tolerate the plundering of those already plundered for the benefit of the plunderer, even though the plunderer had the consent of the plundered. Are the victims of this criminal traffic — widows and orphans of the drink-slain husbands and fathers, the families whose homes have been ruined, and the drunkards anxious to reform — to be further punished that the men who have ruined them may be still further enriched?[5]

The PPA argued that since alcohol was the primary cause of crime, pauperism, insanity and premature death, there was no basis in morality for compensation.

The strongest reason to support prohibition, however, was the war. Canada was engaged in a duel to the death, and the use of liquor appeared to strike at the very heart of the war effort. It not only stole precious food; it also distracted and befuddled soldiers and workers. How could a drunken soldier ever train or fight? He became a burden on his comrades and a friend to the "Hun." And work on the home front was disrupted as well, by accidents, costly mistakes and absenteeism. At home, drink brought only "vicious slums, haunts of vices, overflowing jails, lunatic asylums, workhouses, and wrecked and poverty stricken homes." In the country, one could tell a wet community from a dry one simply by looking at the children's feet. In a wet area, it was asserted, the children all went barefoot because the money had gone to the bar.

Even the emerging social sciences were called upon to produce reams of statistics purporting to show the proportional relationship between alcohol and accidents, crime, prostitution, disease and poverty. It was proven that alcohol did not act as a stimulant or warm the body. Rather, it depressed higher mental functions. Drinking also undermined mental health and prevented recovery from injuries.

At a prohibition convention in 1916, a Colonel Warden, commander of the 102nd Regiment, Canadian Expeditionary Force, recounted his experiences when wounded in South Africa during the Boer War. Despite repeated warnings, other soldiers in his hospital wing had freely availed themselves of champagne and whiskey from the cupboards when the orderlies were absent. The drinkers had, according to Colonel Warden, all promptly died in great agony, while he, though more severely injured, had easily survived — thanks to his abstention from alcohol.[6]

Some argued that the brewing industry was actually in league with the hated Germans, or at least manipulated by them. A fiery advertisement from the People's Prohibition Association read:

> The best blood of the Dominion is being splattered all over the hills of northern France. The fathers and mothers gladly give up their sons: girls give up their sweethearts, and wives give up their husbands. The taxpayers dig into their empty pockets, and all wonder what else they can do.
>
> While Patriotism is ablaze from Vancouver to Quebec, what are the rum sellers doing? They are intervening to balk their country's efforts. Did Canada snivel and cringe and stutter and wriggle and crawl concerning this? Not much. . . .

The answer, according to the *Daily Colonist* was "to close the dirty and disloyal dram shop."[7]

The following patriotic verses appeared in the August 19, 1916, edition of the temperance-minded *World:*

> Are We To Do Our Duty by the Empire
> Or Are We To Neglect It?
> Are we to "Be British" indeed, and remove a
> "Greater enemy than the Hun" from our midst?
> Is the Sacrifice made by our soldiers for us
> On the battlefield to be the only sacrifice?
> The Bar or the War? That is the Question of the Hour.[8]

Prohibitionists borrowed from the rhetoric of the labour movement and attempted to portray the brewing industry as a secret gang of bosses conspiring to suck the energy out of the war effort. Under the title "A Saloonless Nation and a Stainless Flag," the PPA battered away:

> Voters, tomorrow will determine the moral status, and the moral destiny of our province. The question is deeper than the liquor question. It is a question of freedom and democracy. Can a great combine such as the Liquor Combine, by the sheer force of its money power, maintain its monopoly and remain as a leech feeding upon our vitals, when every ounce of efficiency is demanded in a world struggle? . . . Every weakening of the home base, such as is caused by the Liquor Traffic, means the postponement of victory, and some extra boys will have to lay down their lives because of our failure at home.[9]

The theme of "protecting" the soldiers proved a most effective tool for convincing the electorate about the need for prohibition.

Despite the heated accusations of a conspiracy among the liquor barons, no evidence of collusion was ever found. On occasion, there was certainly manipulation and skulduggery by both wets and drys in politics, but convincing evidence of a widespread conspiracy between producers, sellers, servers and political rulers has never been produced. Nonetheless, the obstinate myth of a sinister liquor plot was widely accepted by many as late as the 1930s.

Devoted prohibitionists also preached the unlikely notion that, if alcohol could be excluded from people's lives, if only for a few years, they would soon forget its pleasures. The war, they argued, was really a blessing in disguise because it created an opportunity for change and rebirth. Just keep a stiff upper lip, make the sacrifices — and the world would become a better place. Nellie McClung grimly reminded her audience that "without the shedding of blood, there is no remission of sin."[10] Prohibition, it was argued, would deprive people of the evil nectar for a few months, and then former drinkers would find that their addiction had miraculously disappeared. Even the most devoted alcoholic would no longer feel the slightest urge to partake.

There was a nasty tendency during this period to blame immigrants for bringing their supposed racial and cultural defects with them, and one of these supposed defects was the excessive use of alcohol. "Inferior" racial and cultural groups could impede social and economic progress in Canada by spreading these "physical and mental abnormalities." South Eastern Europe was "the home of illiteracy, the breeding ground of blood feuds, racial animosities and religious bitterness." Chinese or some "lower grades of the Greeks" were behind much immoral behaviour. Slavs and Galicians were "addicted to drunken sprees and animalized."[11] Immigrants were accused of blocking prohibition measures, or, at the very least, ignoring them: "Many of the foreigners have yet to be taught the ABC's of temperance.... Beastly drunkenness has been banished from our social life. With some foreigners they do not consider they are having a good time unless they get uproariously drunk."[12] It followed that if these undesirables could be kept out of the country, prohibition would become unnecessary. Many also complained that "foreigners," being mostly single and male, actively thwarted prohibition measures and were the chief customers of prostitutes.

Ironically, another highly addictive drug — tobacco — was seen as essential to a soldier's welfare in wartime. Considerable funds were solicited by civic organizations to ensure that the fighting man at the front got his cigarettes:

> Tobacco is not a luxury but an absolute necessity for the soldiers according to Mr. Francis R. Jones, organizing secretary of the Over-

seas Club, under whose auspices Canada's Tobacco fund is administered. . . . "The first cry of a wounded man," said Mr. Jones, "is for a smoke." While in the trenches with all the nerve-racking accessories, such as shrapnel shells, the men have got to smoke to preserve their health.[13]

In some ways this misplaced enthusiasm was understandable, for cigarettes provided one of the few comforts available to Canada's hard-fighting soldiers. Cigarettes were a recent innovation, which had become cheap and available after the first automatic rolling machines were brought on line in the early 1880s. This was followed by the introduction of milder varieties and improved curing techniques, which made it much easier to inhale the smoke. As with the introduction of spirits two hundred years before, it took many years for the health dangers of this powerfully addictive drug to be widely recognized. However, the Woman's Christian Temperance Union had long campaigned against tobacco, as well as alcohol, and they actively resisted cigarettes for soldiers. This did not go down well in the trenches. Increasingly, the soldiers began to view the WCTU as a prudish club of old ladies living comfortably at home bent on making the soldier's miserable life even more unbearable.

Meanwhile, the wets continued to scoff at the very idea of liquor prohibition. They pointed out that alcohol had been around for thousands of years. How could such an ancient and ingrained custom as drinking alcohol ever be truly eradicated? And making drink illegal meant giving up any control over its use. Regulations governing saloon hours, days of operation, age limits and purity of product would all go out the window if alcohol were pushed completely outside the law. Social and legal structures that encouraged moderation would be replaced by the law of the jungle. And could prohibition be considered truly Christian if it was imposed by force? As the author of *Facts and Figures Against Prohibition: How to Vote* contended, you can prohibit alcohol or other things as much as you like, but in the final analysis it will be up to individuals to make their decision.[14]

Wets were also beginning to raise questions about the vastly expanded police powers that would be necessary to enforce the new law, and the effect such powers would have on personal liberty. Police searches could be conducted on hearsay evidence alone — without a warrant — and an informer would never have to confront the accused. Also worrying was the reversal of the presumption of innocence in court. Such a reversal had little precedent under British law. But perhaps most important, the prohibition law not only forbade public drinking, it also intruded into one's private life. British civil libertarians believed that as long as one behaved properly in public, what a man ate or drank in private was no one's business but his own. The so-called "un-British" nature of prohibition proved to be an enduring weakness. The defence-of-liberty argument had a powerful resonance with soldiers in the trenches who were regularly subjected to barrages of propaganda, assuring them that they were fighting the good fight — for freedom and democracy at home and abroad.

The PPA tried to mollify these public fears, while at the same time railing against the perfidy of the whiskey conspiracy:

A FALSE ALARM
The public are warned against fake tactics of the liquor merchants who are trying to deceive the people that under Prohibition, the police will begin breaking into houses, etc. The facts are that it will be no different than under the Bowser Act, the police can enter homes without a warrant. The clause in that regard is COPIED almost word for word from the law that is now in force. The only difference under Prohibition will be that the police will be able, also, to enter hotels, club rooms, stores etc., and search for liquor. . . .[15]

The prohibitionists capped their campaign with two huge conventions in mid-August 1916, one in Victoria with 7,000 participants, and the other in Vancouver with 12,000. The great temperance preacher Billy Sunday himself was called in to sermonize to enthusiastic crowds. Sunday, an ex-baseball player from Chicago and flamboyant opponent of drink, campaigned tirelessly for prohibition throughout North America. His revivals were huge productions supported by a "Sunday Party" of staff, including a research assistant, vocal soloist, pianist, publicity manager, private secretary, cook, personal masseur, housekeeper, builder of tabernacles, music director and choir.

On the eve of the convention, a newspaper story accused Sunday of being a German spy, in hopes of having him barred from entering Canada by immigration authorities. Sunday indignantly responded: ". . . the whiskey crowd of Canada are as big a lot of liars as they are in the States. . . . Lies, infamous lies."[16] Just where this curious espionage charge originated is unclear, but it stimulated public interest. During his sermon at the Victoria Hockey Arena, Sunday took off his coat, climbed on chairs and tables, threw imaginary baseballs at the crowd, "slid into second," and almost dived into the packed assemblage, while the crowd "cheered him to an echo." Sunday elaborated:

> Selling liquor is worse than murder. The murderer merely destroyed the body; the liquor dealer damned the soul and scarred the next generation. . . . I serve notice on the whiskey gang of Vancouver and Victoria, you cannot put your dirty claws on the throats of the boys of this province, without having the scrap of your lives. . . . I tell you, if there is a heaven for fools, the man who believes in the saloon will be on the front seat, for, if the saloon is not the dirtiest thing on the face of God's earth, the devil ought to be canonized.[17]

The *World* judged the rallies to be a tremendous success, and the Vancouver gathering was glowingly described as the "largest audience ever assembled under one roof in the Dominion of Canada." But the accolades were not universal. The *BC Federationist* could not help sneering at Sunday's antics. A front page story on August 18, 1916, headlined "Billy Sunday Tunes his Tuneful Lay," contained the following stanzas:

> Sweeter than the murm'ring breezes
> Wafted from the balmy South
> Are the tintinnabulations
> Of my automatic mouth.
> How I love its giddy gargle,

> How I love its rhythmic flow
> How I love to wind my mouth up,
> How I love to hear it go.[18]

The story complained as well that nothing was said that "possessed weight or merit," and that Sunday's "mouthings and frothings" were merely the exhortations of an "anti-liquor zealot and fanatic." The reporter also made the telling argument: "Awful tales did he tell of men maddened by liquor, who beat their mother's head to a pulp with sticks of stove wood etc., but he forgot to mention that many deeds equally horrible and to be deplored had been committed by men made insane by other means than liquor, and not the least prolific of which has been religion itself." The paper went on to ridicule the preacher's assertion that the workingman was the main supporter of the bar: "It is safe to assert that there is a smaller percentage of the workers who are addicted to drink, than there is of the class that lives upon their backs."[19]

As the day of the election approached, the PPA left nothing to chance at the ballot box. In a remarkable document entitled *Workers' Manual Prohibition Campaign (Private and Confidential for Prohibition Workers Only)*, the PPA laid out a strategy of calculated intimidation that would be unacceptable today. A "good strong company of dry voters" and others were instructed to arrive at the polling place just before it opened:

> It is often found that women can do better work than men, both in canvassing voters and in every other part of the work. . . . The plan is to canvass every person who has a right to vote [white males only], either approaching the voter personally or in some way finding out how he stands on this prohibition question — whether for, against or neutral. This information should be carefully recorded in the record book. If he is neutral or against, then his reasons, if any, should be carefully considered and a record made for future use. . . .
>
> The neutral voters should receive special consideration. From them our majority will be built up. Too much cannot be learned about them. What is their objection to prohibition? To what lodge or church do they belong? Where do they work? What are their

business or social connections? Are their wives and sisters in favour of prohibition? Have they any close friends on their side? The more of this information that can be obtained the better. Then let each be approached in the wisest possible way. What we need is to have every shot aimed at a definite mark and hit it.[20]

This kind of pressure on voters proved highly effective at putting opponents of the act immediately on the defensive.

Thus the simplistic battle lines were drawn. A marginal movement that had never received much support in the province before 1915 suddenly found itself setting the agenda for alcohol policy. Ideologically impelled, prohibitionists used fears generated by the war to draw up an uncompromising law. There was little thought given to the costs and mechanics of enforcement. British Columbia now seemed destined to take the path of purity.

It should be noted that the actual use of alcohol in the trenches bore little resemblance to the riotous picture painted by the People's Prohibition Association. For the boys at the front, the joyful cry of "rum up" was "the highlight of the day." When the First Canadian Infantry Division arrived in France in February 1915, it was attached to the British line and was routinely issued the same rum allotment as the rest of the troops. The dose was two ounces of potent "SRD" (Special Red Demerara) 186 proof Jamaican rum, at dawn and dusk. Spooned out from a large earthenware jug, the rum had to be drunk in the presence of the NCO to prevent hoarding. What was left was thrown into the mud (or drunk by the officers and old hands). Teetotallers could opt for lime juice or Oxo soup, but few did. In fact, alcohol proved to be an indispensable part of trench culture, and did much to ease the soldier's burden.

The calming and sedative power of drink allowed soldiers to endure terrible sights and privations that would otherwise have been unbearable. Large quantities of strong drink were doled out just before "going over the top" on an assault. During the appalling Battle of the Somme, the jugs were simply left out, and the men could take what they pleased. It was said that the smell of "rum and blood" saturated the air in battle, and some soldiers were so drunk they could barely find their way out of the dugout. Nonetheless, rum allowed exhausted men to sleep on frigid wet ground in the midst of artillery barrages and firefights, and many claimed it gave them immunity from colds and, at the end of the war, the dreaded Spanish Flu. Rum was given as an incentive before, and as a reward after, some difficult task like burial detail or a night raid. It was also used as an emergency anaesthetic when morphine was not available, and for mental breakdown brought on by battle fatigue.

"God's tranquilizer," or a stiff drink, was the best-known treatment for "shell shock," which was little understood at the time. Several years after the war, a British medical officer testified about the condition before a parliamentary commission: "Had it not been for the rum ration I do not think we should have won the war."[22] Men drinking together mutually boosted morale, fostering a spirit of camaraderie and male bonding. Drinking was a rite of passage that separated the men from the boys, the warriors from the greenhorns. It offered a momentary escape from the impossibly grim world of the trenches. Even strict abstainers found it hard to resist. Gordon L. Macintosh wrote to his father from France in January 1917:

> You asked me in a previous letter if the authorities issue rum to the men. Yes, they do, but in such small quantities there is not much danger of it hurting them. It is issued to fellows in the trenches every morning at 'stand-down,' one large tablespoonful to each man. When a fellow has 'stood to' all night in a trench with the rain pouring down, or lain out in a shell hole for hours at a stretch on 'listening post,' he needs something to stimulate him. I know of plenty of cases of men who never take a drink out of the trenches, but who take their rum issue every morning when they are in.[23]

Officers who refused to issue the allotments of SRD faced open rebellion. Victor Odlum, decorated commanding officer of the

Seventh Battalion, came from a missionary background and despised alcohol. But his popularity dropped to "minus zero" in the front-line opinion polls when he tried to withhold the rum ration, and his superiors were finally forced to overrule him.

It must be admitted, however, that drunkenness both on and off duty was common, although not always reported. More members of the Canadian Corps were court-martialed for this infraction than for all other crimes combined. Soldiers showed a remarkable ability to ferret out liquor in rear areas. Wine and brandy were readily available in the French countryside, as was beer and ale in Britain. But it was the SRD rum that was the favourite. One officer remarked in a letter home: "Rum is a great warmer, but it gives us more trouble than almost anything else, and certainly gets more men into trouble out here than its companion and associate — women."[24]

Trench soldiers usually reacted to the prohibition movement with cynicism and disgust. Harold Baldwin, a Fifth Battalion infantryman who lost his leg, wrote a book after the war about his experiences. He had hard words for the teetotalling do-gooders who had no clue about the horrors that he had been through:

> Oh you psalm-singers, who raise your hands in horror at the thought of the perdition the boys are bound for, if they should happen to take a nip of rum to keep a little warmth in their poor battered bodies. I wish you could all lie shivering in a hole full of icy liquid, with every nerve in your body quivering with pain, the harrowing moans of the wounded forever ringing in your ears, with hell's own din raging all around. Any one of you would need a barrel of it to keep his miserable life in his body.[25]

When the veterans finally returned to British Columbia after the war, their bitterness lingered. What had the great sacrifice in France been for, if not the right to have a peaceful glass of beer in one's favourite watering hole?

CHAPTER 6

DEMOCRACY OVERTURNED
The Soldiers' Vote, 1916–1917

THE PURITY ELECTION of October 1916 was a disaster for Billy Bowser's new administration. His so-called "Little New Deal" of tepid mini-reforms had completely failed to obscure the corruption, vice and greed of the McBride/Bowser machine. Voters wanted purity and virtue to win the war and put the ailing province back on its feet. They did not want more of the same old politics. On the question of alcohol it has been said that Bowser was a damp premier — too wet for the drys and too dry for the wets.

The electorate turned out en masse for the Liberals. In a pattern that has become familiar in British Columbia politics, a party that had ruled for too long was decimated by a violent swing of the electorate. From zero seats at the beginning of the year, the Liberals jumped to thirty-seven seats. The Tories plummeted from forty seats to ten, and even Premier Bowser barely held on to his seat. The new Liberal leader, Harlan Carey Brewster, was sworn in as premier on November 23, 1916. A wealthy cannery owner and Baptist teetotaller, Brewster enthusiastically embraced prohibition.

Nevertheless, the real focus of the all-male electorate was not the contest between the political parties, which was a foregone conclusion. Rather, it was the twin referenda on suffrage and prohibition. As an indication of the rising social consciousness in the province, women's suffrage won by a large margin but, ominously, the results of the prohibition referendum were less clear. Male civilians voted strongly in favour of the new law, with 36,490 votes for and 27,217 against, with only the voters of Alberni, Lillooet and Fernie opposing the Act. (Some of these votes were later disqualified, but prohibition still maintained a majority.) Soldiers at home in British Columbia seemed evenly divided, with 3,353 taking the dry option and 3,622 going for the wet side. But several thousand in Europe voted absentee before September 14, and the majority of these chose the wet side. (Not surprisingly, exact figures seem unavailable for some of these confusing tallies.) Nevertheless, the drys remained comfortably in the lead by what was estimated to be a few thousand. However, there were still the 20,000 or so BC soldiers serving in Europe who had not voted absentee, and they held the real balance of power. It was possible that another strong soldiers' showing against prohibition would alter the numbers enough to doom the legislation. A simple majority, one way or the other, would decide the issue.

Both sides had been quick to see the importance of the soldiers' vote, and both sent representatives to England and Europe to advance their causes. The crucial questions of who would be eligible to vote and what standards would be used to ascertain a voter's identity and residence could be pivotal. Months before the ballot, the executive committee of the PPA anxiously wanted to know "... what soldiers will be voted and which; and also what representation of scrutiny we will have upon taking the vote." As a precaution they added five more members to the Soldiers' Vote Committee, and requested $10,000 to send more scrutineers and observers to Europe.[1]

Bowser, however, had already moved with crafty effectiveness.

112 *Sobering Dilemma*

The soldiers' vote would be moulded as needed. Within days of announcing the referendum, he had quietly arranged for the overseas soldiers' ballot to take place in several stages between October and December 31, 1916 — long after the vote at home in British Columbia. This would allow more than enough time for manipulating the results. Soldiers in Europe would be allowed to vote during lulls in the fighting, but the government refused to provide any real safeguards to protect that vote from manipulation or fraud. Although scrutineers would be present when the vote was tabulated overseas, there was no provision for them to be at the actual polling place. It was common knowledge that certain military officers, such as Captain A. Edward Tulk, had been propagandizing among the soldiers for the liquor cause months before the September elections in British Columbia. Tulk acted as the leading lawyer for the Merchants Protective Association, and remained an indefatigable enemy of prohibition to the end. Most disturbing of all, moreover, was that the man placed in charge of collecting and counting the soldiers' vote in Europe was none other than ex-premier Richard McBride, long-time foe of prohibition and now British Columbia's Agent-General in London.

The results of the overseas vote were electrifying. According to McBride, only 812 out of over 8,500 voting soldiers had cast their ballot for prohibition. The soldiers' polls were so lopsided — and once one factored in the soldiers' absentee vote of some 2,000 against prohibition — they overturned the vote at home and threw the total provincial vote to the wets. The province was stunned to discover that the liquor referendum had lost after all. Most of the province's soldiers in Europe apparently never took the time to vote, or were never properly informed about the election and referenda in the first place — but no matter. McBride assured Brewster that all certificates, poll books and other paraphernalia would be shipped to Victoria immediately. With a provincial total of more than 80,000 voters, prohibition in British Columbia had lost by just 822 votes.[2] It is a testimony to McBride's obfuscations that the actual total of voting soldiers in Europe before and after September 14 remains murky to this day.

After all the melodrama and effort, the result of the overseas vote was a tremendous disappointment to the drys — not to mention that it was also somewhat unbelievable. At home, the soldiers had been evenly split, but in Europe the vote was nine to one against prohibition. The numbers simply did not make sense, and stories of voting improprieties in France and England soon began to surface. Temperance groups launched a vigorous protest campaign, feeling — rightly, as it turned out — that the referendum had been stolen from them in Europe. Angry deputations besieged the legislature, demanding a committee of inquiry on the matter.

Premier Brewster was thoroughly nonplussed by this bizarre turn of events and responded cautiously. He hesitated, and then agreed to support a commission, made up of both parties, to be sent to England to examine the soldiers' vote firsthand. In May 1917, the legislature in Victoria passed the Prohibition Overseas Vote Investigation Act, which organized a court-like tribunal to get to the bottom of the matter. But even as the Act was put in place, there was concern that the in-depth investigation could lead to unpleasant legal repercussions for some soldiers when they finally returned home. This was to be avoided at all costs, since it was felt that the soldiers had already suffered enough. Thus, anyone who agreed to testify honestly to the commission was to be spared "all penal actions, forfeitures, punishments, disabilities, and incapacities to which he may have been or may become liable. . . ."[3] However, those who failed to appear, refused to be sworn or to answer questions could be charged with contempt of court.

On June 18, 1917, in the newly completed British Columbia House in London, the group convened its first meeting to investigate the issues of misconduct, corruption and "personation" (impersonation/fraud) in the overseas vote. Three Liberals chaired the commission: David Whiteside, F.A. Pauline and C.F. Nelson. Lawyers R. Lawson Coad and W.D. Bayley represented the prohibition camp, while the Merchants Protective Association fielded the now familiar A. Edward Tulk, leading barrister of the MPA, and Joseph Martin MP, KC. With so many lawyers, the commission quickly took on the atmosphere of a courtroom drama with both sides intent on scoring points. All realized that the fate of British Columbia's prohibition referendum now hung in the balance.

The first question at hand was to check the identity and eligibility of the voters. Mysteriously, no one had been assigned to monitor the official voting records, and the few records that had survived were withheld from the commission. A chartered accountant, Ernest Alfred Helmore, was appointed by Premier Brewster to examine the ballots and offer a summary of his findings. A voters database would have to be completely reconstructed, from the ground up. Mr. Martin, solicitor for the MPA, strenuously objected, demanding the right to examine all pertinent military records and documents firsthand:

> Clearly there is no chance of cross examining. No matter how much I press, the most that Mr. Helmore can say is that he believes it to be correct and he has examined these documents, which I do not doubt; but he might well make all kinds of errors and if we had the documents here we could check them.[4]

During the drawn-out balloting, thousands of soldiers had voted both at the Front and at the Allied hospitals in England. Each had received a large foolscap envelope with instructions clearly printed on the outside. Inside were found two ballots for the referenda: one on women's suffrage and one on the prohibition question. There were spaces for name, unit, rank and residence in Canada, followed by an affirmation of British Columbia residency, to be signed by the voter and his commanding officer. However, a number of important safeguards were not put in place. In particular, a soldier's all-important military number was not required. This number followed him everywhere he went, and was the most efficient way of keeping track of each and every soldier. Furthermore, although the wording of the affirmation oath was stern, many officers did not bother to "swear" their men or put them under oath to establish residency. After the ballots were marked they were then to be sealed in designated cardboard covers and turned over to election officials.

Accountant Ernest Helmore had collected more than 8,500 ballots, and laboriously made up an index card for each, listing every name and number when available. The information on the ballots was then cross-referenced to check for voter irregularities. Helmore noted, "I was of course confronted at the outset with the difficulty that men's numbers were not often given, nor were they required under the Act itself."[5] The accountant estimated that as many as 5,000 of the 8,500 votes cast in the referendum were untraceable. Many names appeared several times, indicating that hundreds of men had voted twice, and some three or even four times. Hundreds of voters were dead, missing, or prisoners-of-war at the time of the vote. More than 2,000 soldiers had voted in the wrong place; hundreds, perhaps thousands of others, were clearly not British Columbia residents at all. Apparently 1,266 of the names appeared to have been invented out of thin air, with no record of any sort to confirm their existence.[6] Significantly, there was never any attempt to correlate soldiers' names with those on the British Columbia voters list from back home, either before or after the ballot. Such a procedure would have established beyond all doubt who was a voting resident and who was not. Bowser clearly never intended the investigation to continue beyond its initial stages.

William D. Bayley, who had sat on the commission for the People's Prohibition Association, described the unfriendly welcome he received from military brass upon his arrival in England to act as a scrutineer. He was discouraged from meeting with the troops and accused by company officers of spreading dangerous propaganda. This charge he vigorously denied: "Owing to the Military Authorities refusing to grant me the names and addresses of British Columbia troops, and finding on my arrival in England that the Military Commanders were very adverse to any political issues being raised in the camps, I have not in any shape or form campaigned on behalf of Prohibition in Great Britain or France."[7] Scrutineers, Bayley knew, had been repeatedly prevented from monitoring the ballot. He complained that military officers had made it impossible for him to oversee the referendum as intended. PPA observers had been kept in the dark about when and where a ballot would be held until the very last minute, making observation impractical. And when evidence of fraud was clearly demonstrated, Agent-General McBride brushed it off, and saw to it that no votes were ever disqualified.

There were also numerous reports that various officers had openly solicited and bought votes with alcohol. Sergeant Major H.A. Douglas, in charge of the balloting in France, had treated fellow soldiers to beer and liquor before the vote, and then ended their tipple with a toast: "To hell with Prohibition!" Other officers failed to seal the marked votes in the required cardboard holders, refused to surrender the holders for counting, and insisted on carrying their load of ballots "loose about the country for several days." When the holders were finally turned in, days late, the previously missing seals were all mysteriously in place.[8]

There had also been much fudging on who was to be considered a genuine British Columbia resident. Senior officers ransacked various battalions, looking for "BC residents," ordering anyone who had even visited the province to vote. One soldier commented, "He [the officer] said it did not matter how long [I had lived in BC] so long as I was in Khaki."[9] Others were advised to vote several times, because their first vote was "no good"; still others were told that they were actually casting additional votes in a completely different referendum.

On the fifth day of the commission's meetings, the group met at Epsom, a complex of military convalescent hospitals south of London, where some of the worst excesses allegedly took place. This allowed the two sides personally to interrogate soldiers whose votes might be questionable. The MPA's solicitor Joseph Martin asked for reassurance with regard to the question that had been hanging over the investigation from the start. Were the men who had voted twice, or had falsely signed affirmations of residency, guilty of a crime if they refused to admit it on the stand? Many who had knowingly affixed their names to false statements would presumably continue to lie, or simply refuse to testify. Would they now be liable for contempt of court charges? Certainly no one wanted to see these young soldiers in prison — the need for cannon fodder at the front was too great. Mr. Coad of the British Columbia Prohibition Movement tried to reassure the commission: "There is such a thing as a joke, and such things as men being young boys. . . ," but no one was "being tried as a matter of life and death."[10] Not surprisingly, the soldiers on the stand did not share this sanguine view.

For the soldiers called to testify, the experience must have been an exceedingly intimidating experience. In the formal, trial-like atmosphere, one man after another seemed to have enormous difficulties in remembering signing anything, or recalling exactly how and when he had voted. Most claimed that they had never read the fine print, but had just scrawled a signature and cast their ballot. Some, like the severely shell-shocked Carl Henry of Vancouver, genuinely could not remember what had happened. When sharply queried about when he had voted, he answered uncertainly, "I should judge probably two or three months after the first vote. I have been blown up, and my mind is not as clear as it used to be in times gone by."[11] Another soldier rebelliously refused to testify at all, his rage apparent to everyone. William Seppy Robertson would neither raise his arm nor swear an oath. When asked if he had a "conscientious objection" to oaths he replied, "No — do not shoot that at me. Do not start that thing. . . . I have had my share of it and come from another part of the country. . . . If a man puts his hand up, there is generally a long smoke."[12] Robertson was excused without a murmur.

Indeed, these wounded soldiers had seen the worst of it. The Battle of the Somme had commenced in July 1916, and the butchery continued throughout the fall. On the first day alone, there were an incredible 54,470 British casualties; 684 Newfoundlanders were killed or injured out of a total of less than a thousand. It was the worst battle in the worst war Canada had ever fought — over 25,000 were killed or wounded along this sombre river. A great tragedy for both sides, this brutal clash accomplished absolutely nothing, since the battlefield remained virtually unchanged. The combined casualties for both sides exceeded more than 1,200,000 troops. The men examined at the Epsom hospital complex were mainly participants in this ghastly bloodbath, still recovering from their wounds. Their reward for participating in some of the worst fighting in the First World War was a courtroom cross-examination over an intoxicant they could readily obtain anywhere in Europe.

This inquiry represented a moral low for both wets and drys. Bowser and McBride's crude falsification of the vote must be weighed against the prohibitionists' determination to drag these long-suffering soldiers into an absurd kangaroo court. Their callous treatment of shell-shocked soldiers demonstrates just how far the drys were willing to go in pursuing their anti-liquor obsession. One can only imagine what these battered Canadian soldiers thought of it all. The well-dressed members of the commission must have seemed like visitors from outer space. They clearly had no understanding whatsoever of the horrific life in the trenches, or of the rebellion even then brewing amidst the mass of Allied soldiery. Three years of slaughter had created a profound sense of disillusionment among the Allied armies. Just months before, large numbers of French troops had thrown down their arms, and deserted. Russia was already in the midst of a revolutionary meltdown, and there were fears that the malaise would spread to the armies of Britain and her colonies as well. It is surprising that the commission was received as well as it was.

As the Inquiry continued, the Agent-General's shady role in fixing the results of the referendum took center stage. Particularly disturbing was the cozy relationship between A. Edward Tulk and McBride, which blossomed in London during the fall of 1916. Bayley suggested that Tulk had connived with the Agent-General to overturn the referendum.[13] Although no solid evidence could be produced at the time to prove his allegations, the dark suspicions lingered.

The commission held its last meeting on July 11, 1917, and ten days later began the arduous journey home to make its report to the British Columbia legislature. Atlantic convoys still faced a formidable threat from U-boats, and once they reached Canadian shores, the members of the commission had to endure a long railroad trip to the west coast. A special meeting of the legislature was scheduled for August 14 to hear the commission's report, which would finally settle the issue. Although the findings had not yet been made public, news leaks of the many abuses led the wets to prepare for the worst.

In a desperate bid to avoid the inevitable, Tulk applied to the provincial Supreme Court to have the results of the first discredited soldiers' vote certified and published in the *British Columbia Gazette*. He protested that certifying the results of the referendum certainly did not confer "finality" upon the "subject matter." Rather, he was merely following the instructions of Section 11 of the Prohibition Act, which called for publication of the results of the referendum. He added:

> The prohibition party committee never intended to be satisfied with an adverse result. They demanded a referendum because they believed they would receive a majority vote in their favour. Now that it has turned out otherwise they demand a war measure. Instead of waiting for the official report of the overseas commission they have published and criticized parts of the evidence received in order to sway popular opinion and lay the foundation for another demand upon the Legislature. Such conduct has been described as "the justice of Tiberius," and I think it is well deserved.[14]

This clumsy ploy went nowhere.

When the commission arrived in Victoria, its findings completely discredited the soldiers' overseas ballot. With all of the duplications, irregularities and fraud clearly documented, it became impossible to let the vote stand. Of the 8,500 votes cast in Europe after September 14, 1916, a total of 4,697 were rejected because of "irregularities."[15] Three days later, in yet another crazy spin of the wheel of fate, the prohibition law was given final reading in the House — eleven months after the original referendum. The law would come into effect on October 1, 1917.

Scrutineer W.D. Bayley publicly exonerated the soldiers of all responsibility for the debacle, and placed the blame squarely on pernicious liquor interests. He predicted growing support for prohibition in the very near future, as its many benefits trickled down through society:

> Who did the dirty work? Do you think it was the soldiers or the fifty-eight dead men because someone put in their name? Do not blame the soldiers because of the fictitious ballots or the ballots that were torn up. But we are accusing certain agents of the liquor traffic of plugging [bribing] and robbing the men who have gone overseas to fight for us, of their franchises. . . .
>
> The boys coming back will be tired and they will want a big blowout. . . . They will have a little money with them. The best thing you can do for them is to make conditions here such that they will have a chance to keep a little of their money for a fresh start. It is up to us to see that these bloodsuckers of the liquor traffic don't get the chance to bleed our returning soldiers of every cent they have.
>
> Three months after you have had prohibition here there will be a great swing of men who opposed prohibition, but who, having seen it working will swing to the other side to help support the Government and its enforcement and carrying it out.[16]

Ironically, although the soldiers' vote was certainly tampered with, the vast majority of the province's soldiery in Europe had little sympathy for prohibition. Many of those discredited ballots were legitimate and deserved to be counted. British Columbia had the highest rates of enlistment in Canada, and by the war's end more than 55,000 had volunteered for the Canadian Expeditionary Force. There was probably up to 25,000 British Columbians serving in Europe at any given time, but only 8,500 actually participated in the referendum. If all British Columbia solders in Europe during the period 1916 to 1917 had voted, the prohibitionists would have certainly lost in the province. Interestingly enough, a soldier's vote was not even considered in the prohibition referendums in Ontario, Quebec, Nova Scotia and New Brunswick. Hundreds of thousands were effectively disenfranchised — most of them young drinking males. Excluding such a large percentage of the active population did not bode well for the future of prohibition in the rest of the country.

In Victoria, Conservatives and Liberals lined up in favour of the Prohibition Act, with only R.H. Pooley of Esquimalt making a show of opposition. He lamented the "un-British" failure of the government to address the compensation issue, and asked that the date of enforcement be moved from October 1, 1917, to January 1, 1918, to allow merchants time to dispose of their liquor supplies. Otherwise, stocks "would literally have to be thrown in the sewer" to meet the deadline. Premier Brewster impatiently noted that the delays had gone on for long enough, and that the legislature had clearly given its mandate.

In the weeks leading up to October 1, the newspapers were filled with sad and increasingly desperate advertisements as the liquor and brewing companies sold off inventory. The Silver Spring Brewing Company darkly warned, "Prohibition will be here October 1, govern yourselves accordingly." Pither and Leiser published full-page "Public Warning" ads. The Victoria-Phoenix Brewing Company noted, "Our stock is rapidly diminishing. We advise the public to stock up at once on our justly celebrated Phoenix Beer, XXX Ale and Invalid Stout. Imagine Christmas without Phoenix Beer." The liquor store of R.P. Rithet & Company emphasized the countdown: "Only three weeks more before prohibition takes effect. Have you seen to your supplies?" It is said that British Columbia produced some of the finest brews in Canada in the early years of the century. On October 1, that era ended and many of those much-loved brands disappeared without a trace. The *Province* sent a reporter into downtown Vancouver to assess the public mood:

> At 10 o'clock practically every house [bar] closed its doors and there was a little cheering and singing of Auld Lang Syne but the scenes were nothing like the wild excitement of New Year. The late cars carried home the men who had been doing their shopping, and it was noticeable that some were carrying decanters, jugs and other bar supplies. Altogether the old regime passed out with dignity.[17]

There was a profound sense of relief in the province once prohibition was in force. Most people were tired of the endless haggling over numbers in the prohibition referendum; it was time to move on. People could concentrate on winning the war now that the question was finally settled. Or was it? The margin of victory for the entire province was very slender, with a majority of only a few thousand out of nearly 80,000 ballots cast. Were people really ready to give up this age-old pastime and embrace prohibition over the long term — even after the war was won?

As a curious epilogue to the overseas soldiers' vote, four years later an incriminating telegram was leaked in the BC legislature, which suggested that McBride and Bowser had indeed connived to fix the referendum. In 1920, Liberal Attorney-General John Wallace deBeque Farris dramatically read before the House a wire purportedly sent by Premier Bowser to Agent-General McBride in the fall of 1916. Bowser cabled, "The soldiers' vote may give us twelve to fifteen seats. I want 180. Slump general everywhere. Prohibition carried by over 7,000."[18] This terse message sounds very much like a veiled set of instructions, and McBride, it would appear, produced the required results. It had been the soldiers' vote in the provincial election that had allowed Bowser to squeak by in his Vancouver South riding by only twelve votes; and, overseas soldiers provided over 7,500 votes to kill the Prohibition Act. But by 1920, the incriminating telegram was no longer seen as politically relevant. The war was over, and McBride had died in London three years before of Bright's disease. Still, the accusation stung, and Bowser, now leader of the opposition party, indignantly claimed that the ambiguous cable had been "filched" from the Agent-General's personal files. It had been taken completely out of context:

> When that cable was sent they had been some days counting the vote there and I said I was 180 behind. There was another cable, which my friends opposite did not apparently get, telling Sir Richard that Mr. Ross was elected. Naturally we were anxious to know how

the vote was going and we thought he might keep us posted as to how it stood and whether I was elected or Mr. Ross was holding his election. In reality I was elected by the soldiers' vote in Canada, and there was no necessity for my suggesting that I needed further votes there.

That is the explanation for that cable. There was no suggestion that Sir Richard was to see that 180 votes were to be counted by me. I knew Sir Richard McBride well enough to know that such a suggestion would be an insult to a man of his high standing. I must congratulate my friend on having succeeded in having extracted this private cable from the private files of a deceased man.[19]

Bowser, however, offered no explanation for the discredited and lopsided soldiers' vote, which had come so close to sinking prohibition.

CHAPTER 7

THE SECRET FILES OF THE BRITISH COLUMBIA PROVINCIAL POLICE

THE BRITISH COLUMBIA Provincial Police have had a long and distinguished history in the province. Organized in 1858 to bring order during the tumultuous Fraser River gold rush, the force demonstrated from the first a high degree of professionalism and esprit de corps. Many of the recruits were ex-British military officers and others were from a "superior station in life." They quickly brought order to the gold fields and became the official arm of the law in the colony. BCPP officers wore no uniforms until 1924; they lived in the communities they policed, and eschewed the military barracks lifestyle of the federal North West Mounted Police (NWMP). In later years, the Provincial Police became the enforcer of choice for the government in power, and the force was used relentlessly against union strikers and Asian minorities — and to enforce the liquor laws against First Nations people. Although such enforcement was supposed to be a federal responsibility, there were few NWMP officers available, and the BCPP often acted in their place. It made little difference anyways, since supplying liquor to Natives could be either a federal or a provincial offence.

Over the years, the Provincial Police grew along with the province, expanding into fourteen districts with dozens of detachments. In 1887 there were 44 members, in 1904 — 86; in 1911 — 186; in 1917 — 227; and in 1922 — 153.[1] However, these numbers do not show the whole picture, since 90 percent of the province's police forces in 1920 were not Provincial Police at all. Rather, they were municipal police working for the cities and small towns of the province.

The BCPP had particularly close ties with the police forces from the larger towns like Vancouver and Victoria. The rivalry that characterized relations between the NWMP and BCPP did not extend to municipal police forces. Strictly speaking, the Provincial Police had jurisdiction anywhere in the province, but in practice they usually deferred to the city forces and turned suspects over to them for the laying of charges. Similarly, when they pursued illicit distillers, the suspect would be turned over to federal inspectors, who would make the charge since distilling was a federal crime.

As was seen earlier (Chapter 2), disrupting the liquor smuggling rings that supplied Natives along the coast became a major preoccupation for the Provincial Police. In 1895, BCPP Superintendent Fredrick Hussey pleaded for a new powerboat to provide coastal communities with better protection. He complained that properties in these communities were ". . . more or less a prey to wandering whiskey peddlers and smugglers who infest our shores." Hussey claimed that the BCPP saw to it that penalties for infractions of the Indian Liquor Act were "very heavy and rigorously enforced. . . . I am pleased to be able to report that in all other respects our Indians are peaceable and law-abiding and that breaches of the criminal law amongst them are rare occurrences. They are self-supporting and industrious."[2]

Although the BCPP were exempted from military service, when

war broke out in 1914, many joined up anyway, creating a severe shortage of skilled policemen at home. To make up the shortfall, game wardens were also granted military exemption, and were sworn in as official BCPP provincial constables. Suddenly these warden appointments became extremely valuable — as an escape from army service, as a reward to supporters, and as a saleable commodity on the open market. As a result, the quality of the police force took a nosedive. At a time when the overburdened Provincial Police most needed good men, they found themselves attracting people who were ill-equipped for the responsibilities of a police force. In 1915, the chief constable in Golden reported problems he had with the new recruits. In one case he had noted that there were a number of suspicious Austrian and German residents in the area, and that troop trains frequently passed nearby. He left two "Specials" to guard the railway bridge until the last train came through. When he returned, they were both drunk and lying senseless in the snow, unaware that a train had even passed by.[3]

The war also brought many new responsibilities and burdens to the force. The War Measures Act decreed that all German, Austrian and Turkish residents in Canada had to register with their local police. Internment camps for security risks were set up at Vernon, Nanaimo and Morrissey. Railway lines, bridges, wharves and other sensitive areas had to be guarded. Someone also had to respond to the hysterical reports of suspicious aliens, strange lights offshore, German spies, and skulking saboteurs. Responsibility for all of these duties would fall to the Provincial Police. The added burden of enforcing prohibition would make their job all the harder. "Pursuing bootleggers is going to be a massive task" was the grim assessment. Many members were drinkers themselves, lived in the local community, and were simply unwilling to turn in friends and neighbours. From within the ranks of the BCPP itself, there were early doubts that the law would be workable. One retired member recalled:

> Although we were theoretically barred from having an opinion about Prohibition or any political issue, we of course did, and I don't know anybody, teetotaller — and there was quite a few of us

who took pride in not drinking — or drinker, who thought the Prohibition legislation was beneficial or enforceable. Most were sympathetic to the small hotel owners who were being forced out of business and some supervision of how the liquor was disposed of was cursory, particularly since the government was so slow about making payments to the poor blokes. Quantities of wines and liquors were listed as "given away" on the licence claim forms but most of that was probably used to stock private cellars at cost.[4]

The unfairness inherent in the prohibition law made enforcement difficult, particularly in rural towns.

After the war's end, the Provincial Police found themselves facing a completely new set of problems, which left little energy for liquor enforcement. Economic depression, inflation and unemployment had created an ugly labour climate. Wartime inflation had surged, and between 1916 and 1917 the cost of living had jumped by an incredible 30 percent, while union membership had doubled. British Columbia had the reputation for the highest number of radicals per capita in Canada. Organizations like the Vancouver and Victoria Trades and Labour Council overwhelmingly voted for a strike to free political prisoners and to institute a Soviet economic system. Labour organizer Ginger Goodwin was shot down and killed near Cumberland by Dominion Special Constable Daniel Campbell, and strikes paralyzed Princeton, Vancouver Island and the East Kootenays. There were rumours of bomb factories and planned Bolshevik riots on the west coast, and talk of intervention by the NWMP if matters got out of hand. The BCPP kept a close watch on unions, radicals and the Red Menace with spies and informants, but the revolution never materialized.

The winter of 1918–1919 saw the devastating arrival of the Spanish influenza. Fifty thousand Canadians died, millions fell ill, and civic government was stretched to the breaking point, particularly in rural areas. Conventional wisdom had it that alcohol was the only sure preventive for this scourge. One cannot help wondering how these officers reconciled the draconian laws against alcohol with liquor's supposed flu-fighting capabilities.

There is also the larger question of how the BCPP went about their duties when it was clearly so difficult to enforce the provisions of the Prohibition Act. In this regard, it is fortunate that some of the official police records relating to prohibition have been preserved in the British Columbia Archives in Victoria. This important material provides a brief but fascinating glimpse into the inner workings of a police force under considerable stress. The most striking feature is how little material actually survived over the years, for the paper trail of the British Columbia Provincial Police seems almost non-existent. Their prohibition files for 1917 to 1926 consist of only four boxes, many of them full of bureaucratic "certificates of conviction," listing charges and sentences, with few additional comments. There are some monthly summaries of court rulings, which give a good idea of how the courts were coping with the situation. One will look in vain, however, for evidence of the many complaints that grew about problems within the police force itself. As prohibition began to unravel in British Columbia, these records remained predictably silent. There are no records of disciplinary measures against errant constables, and nothing on payoffs, enforcement guidelines, or even officers drunk on the job. Incredibly, there is absolutely nothing documenting the shocking scandals that absolutely discredited prohibition in 1919.

Powerful bureaucracies are not in the habit of saving embarrassing or incriminating documents. Clearly, these files have been vetted many times — not only to save space, but to sanitize. To a certain extent, this is only reasonable. It would have been impossible to save every BCPP report and record for posterity — a dozen warehouses would have been filled to overflowing. Police work has always generated a mountain of paper, which leads us to that critical question facing all historians: What is history and what is junk? One cannot save everything. And yet, police files, in particular, should always be preserved whenever possible, for such materials show what really preoccupied society's leaders at the time: fears — real or misplaced — aspirations and values. Words and speeches tell us what politicians wanted us to believe about themselves and

▲ *"Do you want a bottle or a case?"* Travelling bootlegger displaying his many wares, with shotgun for protection. Near Kelowna, c. 1920. (COURTESY BC ARCHIVES, D-09644)

▶ Seven carcasses of dressed hogs stuffed with bottles of contraband liquor, seized at Tête Jaune Cache, BC, c. 1910. (COURTESY GLENBOW MUSEUM, NA-2651-1)

▲ Working women hold a "drinking bee" at Whitechapel in Dawson City's red-light district during the Klondike gold rush. Their names are lost to history except for Madame Brunell on the left.
(COURTESY YUKON ARCHIVES, MACBRIDE COLLECTION, 3795, LARS AND DUCLOS PHOTOGRAPH)

▲ Sir Richard McBride (Premier of BC, 1903–1915) strongly resisted the calls for local liquor control and provincial prohibition for many years. Later, as BC's Agent-General in London, he manipulated the overseas soldiers' vote on prohibition in the 1916 "Purity Election."
(COURTESY BC ARCHIVES, A-01413)

▲ William Bowser (Premier of BC, 1915–1916) was known as "the Little Kaiser." Like McBride, he personally opposed prohibition. Here he is shown holding court for the Daughters of Pity at a garden party at his residence, c. 1919. (COURTESY BC ARCHIVES, A-06781)

▶ The 29th (Vancouver) Battalion, Canadian Expeditionary Force at Albert on the Somme, France, voting on prohibition in the BC provincial elections of 1916. (COURTESY CITY OF VANCOUVER ARCHIVES LP202 MILP258N100)

▲ A final toast and fond farewell to drink in Silverton on the eve of prohibition, October 1917. (COURTESY BC ARCHIVES, F-02383)

▲ Bar in Prince George, c. 1919, wrecked by returning veterans unhappy with prohibition. (COURTESY BC ARCHIVES, D-07329)

their policies; police work shows us what they really cared about. Sadly, the material contained in the archive must be seen as only a tiny fraction of the whole. Despite the fragmentary nature of the material, however, an occasional gem shines brightly for the discerning reader.

In the first few weeks of prohibition, wholesale confusion reigned at the BCPP headquarters in Victoria. Things improved only slightly over time. The Prohibition Act was strict but unclear in some critical particulars. A myriad of questions and complications confounded the police, who were forced to immerse themselves in a Kafkaesque world of legal nitpicking. For example, all agreed that it was perfectly legal to possess alcohol in a "private dwelling." But much of the province's workforce lodged in cabins, trailers, bunkhouses, float houses, tents and even boats. The Superintendent of Police commented: "A cabin with a bed and stove in it is not a private dwelling house within the meaning of the Act. The Act requires something further than that. There should at least be facilities therein for cooking and the family should actually reside, cook, sleep and take meals therein."[5]

A boat or trailer was a conveyance and certainly not a dwelling. In effect, this made possession of alcohol illegal for most low-income workers. If found guilty, one faced a fifty dollar fine plus costs, or thirty days' hard labour.

A confused grocery store owner inquired whether stores were banned from selling Natives vanilla extract with a 1 percent alcohol content — which was still legal for whites. The Superintendent replied in a letter, "I know of nothing to prevent you, but if the Indians supplied with these beverages stated they became intoxicated by drinking them you might be liable to prosecution under the Liquor Act."[6]

The Leach River Hydraulic Mining Company applied for an allowance of one pint of ethanol a week for cleaning gold. At first the Provincial Mineralogist advised the Superintendent that he was unaware of "any means of cleaning gold or dissolving grease with alcohol." In fact, this had been a common practice for centuries, and after a flurry of letters making this clear, the allowance was granted.[7]

Some of the more interesting items to have survived the years are the letters from informants among the general public. In almost all cases, these were signed and indicated a sincere desire to curb demon alcohol. But the letters hinted at serious problems within the police force itself, and many demonstrated a nasty happiness in tattling on neighbours. Certainly the grammar, spelling and punctuation suggest authenticity. P.J. Hamlin wrote:

> Mr. Farris, Attorney-Gen.
>
> It is about time some one should be looking into the way things are at the Goldstream Hotel. I do not say they sell liquor but it looks that way by the Drunks you will see there and also by the gay bunch that gathers there and the way they act on the road when going home.
>
> I think if you put a private man there will be no trouble in getting them. There is no use to say anything to the Police especially Mr. Olson as he will tell her so things can be moved. Saturday nights and Sundays is the time to get the place.
>
> I do not wish my name brought up as I work for the E&N and they do not care for their employees to get mixed in outside affairs.[8]

It is perhaps an indication of the lack of response on the part of the police that Mr. Hamlin felt obliged to send a second letter two months later:

> Dear Sir,
>
> Some time ago I asked you to have a eye on Goldstream Hotel so far there has been nothing done. I feel if there was any watching done this place could be closed up. Now there is going to be a big time there May 22nd. If you will have this place watched for a day or so I am sure you will get them. The crowd that goes there evenings and comes away from there is not a fit thing to have on the Road. I cannot say if they get their booze there or bring it with them. but I am paying taxes and have a right to demand this thing looked into. It is no use to send Policeman Olson there, as he tells Mrs. Wilson all that is going on and she says she has the bunch on her sheet so,

you will have to work some other way, but you surely will be rewarded if it is looked after. I hope you will see to this.[9]

In fact, the Goldstream Hotel and the Four Mile House on Goldstream Road were both raided and searched on several occasions, but little was ever found.

Sometimes it seemed like the settling of personal feuds was as important to the writer as the stopping of liquor sales. Indeed, many of these letters give the impression of tattletales simply trying to get their enemies and rivals in trouble with the police. This from Mr. K. Johnston in Hope:

> Mr. — Findlay Pro — Commissioner
> Dear Sir,
>
> I find I have lost your address so will have to send this in care of the *World*. I want you to send some one to investigate the liquor conditions in Hope. It is said to be an open fact known to all the people liquor is being sold in the hotel freely, and I am satisfied it is being sold in the Drug Store, the owner being under the influence of liquor very often I have seen and heard men there three or four at a time leaving at late hours near midnight on Sunday night.
>
> Also at a Real Estate Office, Mr. Wendt's they gamble and drink I believe until all hours Sunday night they are there until very late always card playing and I am told they drink and keep liquor there.
>
> If you can send someone unknown to the men he can easily get all the evidence he wants I am confident in all three places. If he does not let them know what he is after.
>
> You can depend on J. Smith at the Post Office or W. Jones for information but they don't wish to be known as informers perhaps. I don't know just how the Police below stands but he appears to be friendly with all parties and I don't think he would want to be the officer to catch the guilty parties. That is only because he does not do it as he might anytime if so disposed. I hope you can do something very quickly and that the lesson taught wont be easily forgotten. Hope needs a severe lesson.
>
> P.S. If they knew I put you into this they won't have much use for me.[10]

The problem of what to do with confiscated alcohol presented a particularly daunting problem. The police lock-up at first seemed the ideal place to store it, but liquor and criminals make for a bad combination, as the following letter indicates:

Supt. of Provincial Police Victoria, BC
Re Confiscated liquor

Sir: — I wish again to draw your attention to the advisability of having this liquor removed from Princeton Lock-up.

Last night we had a bunch of drunks run in, and as we had a man under sentence, we placed him in the cell and left the others in the corridor, during the night they contrived to reach into the cell where the liquor is stored and by the aid of a screw tapped one of the kegs and were all dead to the world this morning.

I think it would be a good idea to take the kegs out and knock in the heads for they have been nothing but a source of trouble ever since they were seized, and the sooner we get rid of the infernal stuff the better pleased I will be.

I would greatly appreciate your advice in this matter.

I have the honor to be, Sir, Your obedient servant, J.A. Fraser Chief Constable.[11]

A similar problem arose in Vancouver the same year, but this time it appears the police authorities themselves were the liquor thieves. Certainly, the value of quality liquor shot up immediately after prohibition came into force in late 1917. With wages of less than twenty dollars a week, some members of the BCPP were tempted to make a little money on the side selling confiscated booze:

I may say that I am assuming no responsibility in connection with the custody of this liquor [seventy-five cases of valuable rye whiskey in the lock-up] seeing that there are so many keys for these cells. However, Mr. Preston of the Supreme Court registry has placed a Yale lock on these cells, so that our Department have no responsibility.

S.R. Dunwoody, Deputy Inspector, Vancouver[12]

Undercover officers were soon enlisted in the war against liquor. These secret agents or "operatives," as they came be called, would attempt to buy a bottle or even a drink from suspected bootleggers and then report them to the police. The use of informants and plainclothes "dry squads" for arrests became much more prevalent after 1920 when American prohibition created a huge illicit bootlegging industry in British Columbia and the government was forced to clamp down. A constable describes his plans for entrapment at a logging operation in Shawnigan Lake in 1920:

> I know at one time this Chinaman was selling liquor, but from information I have received recently he has stopped. . . . However, if I can get one of the loggers to buy a bottle, I will do so, as I warned the Chinaman at the time of the searching.[13]

Letters were also written full of misinformation to throw police off the track. The assumption was that if the police would be persuaded that everyone was peaceably obeying the law there would be no need for police interest:

> Re ASHCROFT:
> Col. J. Sclater, Prohibition Commissioner, Victoria, BC
> Dear Sir:
>   There is no room for improvement in the enforcement of the Prohibition Act in Ashcroft. The Provincial Policeman stationed there is very strict and active.
>   About a month ago he arrested the Proprietor of the Bar in the Ashcroft Hotel and the Court fined him $50.00 for selling draught beer of prohibited strength, (am told 7%) the draught beer now sold, [is] not above legal strength.
>   The Policeman does not even permit pool playing after 11:00 p.m., and questionable looking women getting off the train are warned to get out of town on the next train and they obey without question.
>   Residents with whom I spoke were glad Ashcroft is still unorganized and so enjoy good law enforcement and low taxes under Provincial Government control.
>   Respectfully, "Agent X"[14]

In fact, another letter, dated December 11, indicates that Agent X was a trickster — Ashcroft was wide open, as the following letter makes clear: "My informant states the Provincial Police cannot be ignorant of the condition so many are getting it and drunkenness is rife." Booze was being "sold openly" from the hotel soft drink establishment.[15]

It seems clear that some towns managed to ignore the prohibition law entirely. Municipal police would have a working arrangement with their counterparts in the BCPP and RCMP to notify locals in advance of a raid or visit. An ex-coalminer from Cumberland describes the connection:

> I sold beer in the King George Hotel on Sundays. When a Mountie was coming to town he had to notify the city policemen. So as soon as the city policeman got to hear that the Mounties were coming, he'd phone the hotel and say, "Don't sell anything today."
>
> We had our own police and the bar was open on Sunday. Nine o'clock they used to open on Sunday morning. The one you had to watch for was the Union Hotel because that was outside the city and the RCMP used to come down and look in the door so we'd keep the door locked. But the Waverley and them, they'd keep the door wide open, city police, our own police, we'd can the bugger if he did anything. He was scared.[16]

Emancipated women drinkers posed a special problem for police. In the early years of the century, women were rarely seen in bars or inebriated in public. By 1917 they were smoking in public, driving motorcars, and shamelessly showing a fondness for drink. "Women are going to require more policing than in the past and that means we have to develop more adequate policies and instructions of how to police them," was the judgment of Superintendent McMynn. Searching a woman's clothing for hidden liquor had to be a delicate process since there were no female constables at the time. In many cases police took the chivalrous path and refused to press charges. Such was the case with a "respectable" lady stopped for reckless driving. She was identified as the wife of a prosperous shopkeeper and readily admitted a fondness for whiskey. When the constable took a look in the backseat he discovered four one-gallon tins of the liquor. In triumph, he brought the woman down to the station for arrest and booking. Much to her amusement, his senior officer ordered her taken home instead, and no charges were ever laid. The woman was later placed under the care of a physician, a common practice in dealing with errant woman drinkers.[17]

The certificates of conviction contained in the archive give only a fragmentary evidence of the nationality, race, sex and place of conviction of offenders. For some periods, Vancouver, Victoria, and various interior towns are not even included in the files. Certainly the vast majority of convictions were for "possession" in a place other than one's home, which carried a fine of fifty dollars or thirty days. Very few received the far stiffer six months of mandatory hard labour for "selling," which was imposed on hardcore, second-and third-time offenders.

For the police and the courts, the line between possessing liquor and providing it to others must have been very fine indeed. How could one tell who was the owner of the bottle in a crowd of festive violators? Interestingly enough, public drunkenness was not considered a violation of the Prohibition Act unless one had illicit liquor in one's possession at the time of arrest. Fines of $100 to $400 were handed down occasionally, but judges seemed to restrict the higher fines to those few who could pay. Hotels and breweries caught selling real beer were treated severely, being fined "$1,000 or distress" — which meant they were forced to come up with the money or sell their equipment and go out of business. But as a result of near universal flouting of the law, only a small minority were ever charged.

The law was also erratically enforced. During some months the courtrooms seemed almost empty, whereas at other times there were dozens of convictions. The first few months of prohibition were the harshest, with several hundred convicted during the December/January holiday season of 1917–1918 alone. By the end of 1918, there were fewer of the six-month sentences being handed out, and more fifty dollar fines for possession. Periodic police crackdowns soon took the place of steady and strong enforcement.

When the criminal justice system refuses to enforce a law consistently, the legislation falls into a dead zone in which it is still on the books but is discredited. An unfortunate side effect was selective enforcement. The law's use became dependent on the personal whim of the police, who let their own prejudices get in the way. They became police, judge and jury all rolled into one. If the constable did not like an individual's race, religion or looks, a minor liquor offence could suddenly become serious. The BCPP and municipal police had never been trained for such duties, and their credibility suffered. Signs of unfairness undermined the prohibition law and reinforced the view that it had a class bias.

Furthermore, there was a major discrepancy in sentencing. Some of British Columbia's interior towns were bone dry, and even minor violators were shown little mercy. During June 1919, the strict judge in Fernie sentenced eight violators to six months' hard labour, while only two other people in the entire province received the same treatment that month.[18] If one had to be arrested, clearly it made much more sense to be collared in a big city like Vancouver or Victoria, rather than a country backwater.

And it also helped to be white. Again, statistical analysis is difficult, for the files are incomplete. Last names are the only clue to race. Many of the smaller stores were owned by Chinese, Japanese and East Indians, making them particularly vulnerable to harassment. Still, one sees many Asian names on those Certificates of Conviction, and many other records show a strong preoccupation with "foreign elements." In Victoria an undercover constable was sent to the Ming Chong Company and H. Shirato's store to try to purchase illegal refreshments, but they would sell him only nearbeer. He noted in his report, "It was impossible to obtain any information against either of these stores as the racial prejudice against Orientals was so strong that neither whites nor breeds would attempt to get even a drink from them."[19] Use of what would today be considered derogatory racial slurs were common in reports. Mixed-race Natives were "breeds," Asians were "chinamen," and hard-drinking Italians were "dagos."

Almost no court transcripts of prohibition cases have survived, but for some mysterious reason a few were preserved in the police files. Typical was the case of Bill Lee, a Chinese restaurant owner in Nakusp, charged with selling liquor from the back room of his restaurant to one David Jones. Jones had recently moved to Nakusp and found work in the Silver River Lumber Yard. He boarded at a nearby restaurant and store owned by Lee and tended by Mrs. Elda Phelps. In his testimony before two Justices of the Peace, Jones admitted buying liquor from Mrs. Phelps at the store on several occasions. During the Christmas season he offered her $8 for half a bottle of brandy after she had suggested $20 for the whole bottle. (In early 1917, a dozen quarts of Renay and Co. seven-year-old brandy could be had for $13.) The Chinese owner overheard the transaction and advised Mrs. Phelps not to make the sale, as he was afraid that Jones would get too drunk and "give up the game." Mrs. Phelps sold the brandy anyway, and Jones and his pal Peters went outside the restaurant to kill the bottle. Peters, his partner in crime, corroborated most of Jones' story, but refused to testify against the Chinese owner. He admitted lending Jones the money for the bottle, and sharing it with him, but would not implicate either Mrs. Phelps or Bill Lee:

> Question: Did you see David Jones buy this brandy?
> Answer: No.
> Question: Do you know who he got it from?
> Answer: No.
> Question: Do you know where he got it from?
> Answer: No.
> Question: Do you know when he got it?
> Answer: No.

Unfortunately for Bill Lee, an accountant was able to produce a receipt of itemized hotel expenses (Exhibit C) signed by the accused. One of those expenses was clearly labelled "$3.00 for liquor." Lee protested that he had never sold liquor to Jones, and that he had signed the damning receipts in ignorance, without being able to read them because of his poor English. Mrs. Phelps supported her employer and denied everything:

> I never had any brandy at the restaurant. I never saw a Hennesy bottle in my room. I never sold David Jones any brandy or anything like brandy. I never ask him [for] $20.00 for a bottle because I never had a bottle. I saw Bill Lee had liquor on an order from the Doctor about the last week of November or the 1st week of December. I never saw Jones when he had been drinking.[20]

The two Justices of the Peace hearing the case promptly sentenced Bill Lee to six months of hard labour in the Nelson Jail.

This story raises a number of curious questions. Why, among the thousands of court transcripts concerning prohibition was this one preserved all these years? Did the police themselves have some doubts about the justice of the sentence, or was this considered a textbook example of a job well done? It remains unclear who actually owned the bottle. Why wasn't Mrs. Phelps arrested, as she did the actual selling? In fact, Lee clearly tried to prevent the transaction. Was the whole thing a setup by the police to railroad the Chinese restaurant owner into prison? And why did Mr. Jones testify against Mrs. Phelps and Bill Lee in the first place? Had he seen the light about demon alcohol? Did he feel pressure from his employers? Or did the police have something else on him?

In sum, the prohibition files of the BCPP suggest that enforcement of prohibition was fraught with inequities and contradictions. Much depended on who one was, and one's whereabouts at the time of arrest. Convictions were hard to achieve, as few were willing to testify, and the police themselves became increasingly reluctant to uphold the law. They were not alone. Everyone from the provincial attorney-general down to the lowest judge showed continued reluctance to impose the draconian sentences. A hard-labour sentence at the newly opened Oakalla Prison Farm was definitely hard time. The work was chain-gang style, the regime strict, and the food poor. At home, jobs were lost, families suffered, and reputations were destroyed. One ex-member of the BCPP recalled in 1984:

> I think Prohibition caused more problems than it cured. Alcohol was manufactured in the numerous backwoods stills and sold in the second-class joints in towns. Some of it was pretty dangerous stuff.

Owners of such joints would pretend that they made enough to stay open through near-beer sales, but we'd know it was not very likely. I recall finding a large supply of liquors behind a removable panel on a soft drink bar. The senior constable with me poured it all out and told the owner that if he tried to replace it, he'd have to charge him the next time. Guess he should have charged him then but it would have meant six months in jail and a $1,000 fine for the fellow. I think that owner closed the hotel shortly after and moved his family to the Okanagan.[21]

The riddle of the missing files and boxes of the Provincial Police remains puzzling. Whatever became of that paper mountain of early police history? Ex-Deputy Commissioner of the BCPP, Cecil Clark, offered one explanation to the author in an interview in 1989. Clark joined the BCPP in 1917, and reached his senior rank after over forty years of service. He authored *Tales of the British Columbia Provincial Police* in 1973.

As Clark described it, the 1950 transition from provincial to federal policing in British Columbia was not an easy one. Rumours began to swirl in February, when the change was proposed as a cost-cutting measure — members of the RCMP were paid $1,500 a year, while a BCPP constable received from $2,400 to $3,000. Replacing the BCPP with the RCMP would save up to $1,500 per man the first year alone. Six months of silence about the change followed, and then the end came with surprising suddenness. On August 4, 1950, British Columbia's Attorney-General, Gordon S. Wismer, signed a "hush-hush" agreement with the RCMP, effectively ending the ninety-two-year tenure of the provincial police. Twenty-four senior officers were sacked (including Clark), and the remaining 506 rank and file were offered positions with the RCMP — at a significant cut in pay.

But politicians and citizens, as well as the beleaguered Provincial Police were furious, as there had been no consultation with anyone — not even the British Columbia legislature. Words like "raw deal," "high handed," "shortsighted" and "shabby" were used to characterize the changeover.[22] Nevertheless, within ten days, the head of the Alberta RCMP had installed himself in Victoria as the new provincial police chief, bringing with him a whole new staff of senior officers.

Relations between the provincial and federal police forces in the province had never been particularly cordial. A nasty competitive rivalry had developed between the two police forces over the years, dating back to the 1880's railway boom. The RCMP's relentless progress in taking over other provincial police forces also did little to promote good will. During the "Dirty Thirties" alone, they replaced the provincial police in Alberta, Manitoba and the three Maritime provinces.

This old feud may explain what is said to have happened next. The first act of the federal force after arriving in British Columbia was to clean house. According to Clark, hundreds of boxes of Provincial Police records, reports, photos and memos were unceremoniously hauled off to the dump in a great bureaucratic cleansing.

CHAPTER 8

CORRUPTION AND SCANDAL
Prohibition Discredited

IN THE WEEKS FOLLOWING October 1, 1917, the optimistic predictions of the prohibitionists seemed to be realized. Public drunkenness, accidents and brawling almost vanished, and several small jails were closed for lack of prisoners. Sixty of the sixty-nine hotels in Vancouver and most of the forty-seven hotels in Victoria remained open selling soft drinks and near-beer. It seemed that the furor about compensation might be irrelevant. In Nanaimo, however, the coal miners were not inclined to accept the weak brew; of eighteen hotels, only a couple were expected to remain open. Hotel rates went up to compensate for lost revenue, while the standard of hotel management deteriorated.[1] The province's single distillery ceased operation but reopened again in 1920.

Retail Christmas sales boomed in 1917, which John Nelson attributed to the extra money prohibition had left in people's pockets.

Similarly, the Victory Bond drives set a record in the year following prohibition. Over 55,000 people applied for bonds, paying out an impressive total of $36,411,915. One in every seven British Columbians purchased a war bond that year, and the average per capita investment reached $91.15. "It was generally admitted the objective was attained because of Prohibition."[2] Sceptics countered by pointing out that drinking had actually fallen steeply after the outbreak of the war in 1914, and they claimed that the prohibition law was actually having a negligible effect on alcohol consumption (see Appendix Table 2).

But the supposed benefits of prohibition soon proved fleeting. As predicted, the special exceptions for the rich became a source of irritation. Wealthy tipplers could always import from out of province. For the impatient, the quickest way to obtain legal booze was through a doctor's prescription. Within a few months, the medical profession had become responsible for the most flagrant abuses of the new law. Physicians raked in huge sums peddling prescriptions to those who could afford them. A patient would arrive in the doctor's office, pay his two to four dollars (a full day's wages) for a certified prescription to be filled at any pharmacy liquor store — no questions asked. In 1919 alone, medicinal liquor outlets and drugstores filled more than 315,000 prescriptions in the province, with some doctors writing more than 4,000 a month.[3] The province's entire population at that time was around 450,000. One resident wryly described the host of illnesses that always seemed to strike right around the holiday season:

> Towards Christmas especially it looked as if an epidemic of colds had struck the country like a plague. In Vancouver queues a mile long could be seen waiting their turn to enter the liquor store to get prescriptions filled. Hindus, Japanese and Chinese varied the lines of the afflicted of many races. It was a kaleidoscopic procession waiting in the rain for a replenishment that would drive the chills away; and it was alleged that several doctors needed a little alcoholic lineament to soothe the writer's cramp caused by indicting their signatures at two dollars per line.[4]

The Prohibition Act had granted the PPA the exclusive right to appoint a "Prohibition Commissioner" to manage the liquor stocks legally available to doctors, industry and churches. This grandly named appointee was to arrange for the importation of liquor, see to its safe storage and organize carefully supervised distribution. He released two reports that shed light on the effectiveness of the law, one in 1920 and the other a year later. The commissioner's findings did not reflect well on enforcement procedures and the medical profession. With hundreds of thousands of phoney booze prescriptions, only thirteen doctors and seven druggists had actually been caught and charged in two years. Convictions for selling were also surprisingly low, at just under 450 convictions. Illegal possession was the most common liquor crime.

PROSECUTIONS FOR THE YEAR 1919		PROSECUTIONS FOR THE YEAR 1920	
For Selling Liquor	89	For Selling Liquor	360
Illegal Possession	663	Illegal Possession	1,318
Against Doctors	9	Against Doctors	4
Against Druggists	5	Against Druggists	2
Against Breweries	11	Against Breweries	2
Against Liquor Companies	0	Against Liquor Companies	5
General Infractions of Act	51	General Infractions of Act	136
Not stated	68	Not stated	0
TOTAL	896	TOTAL	1,827
Convictions (315,177 liquor prescriptions issued)	805	Convictions (141,057 liquor prescriptions issued)[5]	1,691

To combat the multitude of bogus prescriptions, the commissioner called for more forms and regulations. Among the recommended suggestions were the following:
- Make it a criminal offence to traffic in prescriptions, and force the suspected violator to prove his innocence in court.
- Set a "definite limit" for the total amount of alcohol that could be prescribed and the number of prescriptions per week.

- Force all doctors to keep detailed records of liquor prescriptions for at least six months for inspection on demand by the Prohibition Commissioner.
- Limit the number of prescriptions a doctor could issue each month.
- Charge druggists with a criminal offence if they filled prescriptions that were more than two days old, or originated more than five miles from their pharmacy.[6]

Many of these cumbersome restrictions were enacted into law by 1920. Pads of officially numbered prescription forms were issued to all doctors, who were limited to only 100 liquor prescriptions per month. Druggists were forced to reduce their dosage from two quarts to eight ounces, unless the patient lived more than five miles from a government liquor vendor. The new rules reduced the number of liquor prescriptions by more than 50 percent the next year, but the number was still absurdly high at over 141,000.[7]

Particularly galling to the commissioner was the clever counterfeiting of prescription forms. Shortly after the appearance of any new document, talented forgers would mass-produce hundreds of copies: "Towards the end of the year it was discovered that attempts were being made to counterfeit these forms, and steps were immediately taken to have a special watermark paper manufactured, on which these prescription forms could be printed, which would prevent, or at least render extremely difficult, any attempt at counterfeiting being made successfully." Government vendors, druggists, Chiefs of Municipal and District Police, as well as Provincial Police, were told to keep an eye out for these phoney prescriptions and to "educate the druggists" on how to detect them. "The difficulty of proving guilty knowledge on the part of persons presenting these counterfeits . . . made the task of the police in dealing with this situation rather difficult."[8]

Similarly, it became impossible to keep track of hospital and industrial stocks, even as the new anti-liquor machine mushroomed in size. Millions of forms, permits, labels, rules and regulations were printed, with countless courts, boards and committees set up to keep track of it all. A bureaucratic monster had been unleashed.

The commissioner responded to complaints of lacklustre enforcement by pointing out what many saw as a major flaw in the Act — the unusually harsh penalty for the sale of alcohol. Six to twelve months of hard labour, without option of fine, was a crushing sentence, which many magistrates were hesitant to enforce. Humanitarian concerns as well as good sense dictated greater flexibility for sentencing in the courts. The commissioner argued that "the severity of the penalty is thwarting the very purpose it was intended to serve — viz., to prevent the illegal sale of liquor by the conviction and punishment of those who engage in this unlawful practice." He concluded that more convictions could be obtained and prohibition better enforced if magistrates were to impose "a fine for the first offence, and in default of payment imprisonment as is done in other Provinces."[9] Prohibitionists, however, refused to countenance any relaxation of the rules, and the heavy penalties remained on the books until 1921.

Another serious shortcoming of prohibition was the diminution of product purity. There was obviously no quality control for illegal alcohol, but people were still drinking it in quantity. As was the case with prohibition imposed on British Columbia's Natives (and still continuing at this time, of course), alcohol could be anything from the finest imported spirits to deadly antifreeze. Poisonings were common, particularly among the poorer segments of the population. One simply never knew what was really in an illegal bottle. It paid to be cautious. An old Nanaimo coal miner remembers: "A bunch of us got together one time and bought a bottle of the stuff and I took one drink and said, 'That's enough for me, you can have the rest.' A lot of people went blind from drinking that moonshine. Wasn't properly distilled."[10]

Billy Bowser quipped that Johnny Walker had been replaced by a new drink of inferior quality, which he dubbed "Farris whiskey." Liberal Attorney-General John Wallace deBeque Farris, an appointee of Harlan Brewster, was to come under increasing attack for being soft on booze, and was forced to resign from Cabinet under a cloud in 1921. Angry letters began to appear in the newspapers, pointedly blaming the drys for the poisonings

> which have been the cause of many deaths, for which I consider the Prohibitionists are answerable, if not to their fellow men, at least to God. . . . The ramifications of the trade are so multiform, and the secrecy investing illicit manufacture is so profound that the police themselves admit the task of enforcing the law is beyond their means.[11]

Another problem was that both the apparently innocuous 1 percent "beerless" and the 1.5 percent near-beer could be sold to children. It was found that even this small concentration of alcohol was sufficient to make a child drunk if imbibed in sufficient quantity. Attorney-General Farris observed:

> . . . there has been a very general demand from the municipalities of the province that power be given them to license and regulate these places. At the present time, there are no restrictions whatever against the sale of near beer, and I am sorry to say that in these unrestricted sales the beer has a way of becoming a good deal nearer than it should be. There is nothing to prevent even the youngest boys and girls from purchasing and drinking near beer in any of the places vending soft drinks.[12]

It was common knowledge that some breweries stubbornly continued to produce full-strength brew along with near-beer throughout the prohibition period. Whenever the authorities stopped by to check, bottles were switched. When all samples were tested, some exceeded 6 percent alcohol, while others fell in the 4 to 5 percent range.

Meanwhile, the war situation remained grim, with combatants on all sides caught in a deadly stalemate. Pressure grew to move Canada further along the route towards complete prohibition. Ontario had gone dry in March 1916, after 15,000 people demonstrated and presented a petition signed by 825,000 people. Nova Scotia, Manitoba and Alberta had followed the same year. As has been seen, in 1917 it was British Columbia's turn, along with

Saskatchewan, New Brunswick, and Newfoundland. PEI had been dry since 1901.

Robert Borden, the newly elected Prime Minister, had campaigned with promises of complete countrywide prohibition and suffrage. He kept his promise, and the Cabinet passed a flurry of orders-in-council which were consolidated in the spring of 1918 and became effective on April 1. For the first time in history, the federal government had almost, but not quite, shut down the liquor trade in Canada. Citizens were forbidden from inter-provincial trade in any alcoholic beverage stronger than 2.5 percent proof. Production of alcohol was drastically reduced, but not eliminated. Beer, wine and spirits could be brewed to supply the legal domestic trade in medicinal alcohol and, of course, the soldiers' rum ration was sacrosanct.

Liquor could also be manufactured for sale outside of Canada, and possession in small quantities at home was also acceptable. The measure would remain in effect until a year after the war ended. In a spirit of self-sacrifice and patriotism, every province but Quebec went dry for the duration.

With its strong Catholic constituency, Quebec had never completely accepted wartime prohibition. Nevertheless, Premier Lomer Gouin came under increasing pressure to add beer and wine to the prohibited list, and he reluctantly agreed to hold a referendum. Even as Quebec appeared to be moving towards complete prohibition like the rest of the country, a respected Cabinet minister suddenly turned the tables. He called the vote a "Methodist plot" directed against the Catholic Church, with the sole purpose of destroying the sacrament by taking away the wine. Such statements resonated strongly in Quebec, and 78 percent voted against the ban in April 1919. Some polling stations reported zero votes for prohibition.[13] Thus, Quebec became the only province to allow the sale of beer and wine during the final years of the war. However, the new orders-in-council of April 1918 effectively closed the import loophole from Quebec into British Columbia, and left the doctor's office as the only source of legal alcohol in the province.

Then, almost as unexpectedly as it had begun, the war finally ended in November 1918, and with it passed the best reason for liquor prohibition. There were no more food shortages, no more rationing, and no more need to produce mountains of food for the Allied war effort. In fact, prices for almost all commodities crashed dramatically after the Armistice, which created economic stagnation and depression. Under the Dominion laws, strong drink remained illegal in Canada, but many people began to take up their old bad habits. With the guilt of undermining the war effort no longer a factor, why should drinkers continue to abstain? The old moral arguments proved too weak to maintain support for this unpopular law. Liquor prohibition in British Columbia had been in effect only a little over a year, and now in late 1918 it began to unravel as more and more people ignored the law.

The drys blamed the police for lax enforcement, and they were right. A large deputation of lay and clerical prohibitionists met with the Board of Police Commissioners in December 1918 to voice their criticisms. Booze, they claimed, was available in bars in Victoria "almost as freely as in pre-prohibition times." The only difference was that the "liquor now is higher in price and lower in quality." There were more intoxicated men in the streets, and near-beer was being replaced in hotels by a strong beer of 5 to 6 percent. "Oh, there is no doubt a man can get a drink day or night" grumbled Reverend Stevenson. The situation had got so bad that several Victoria near-beer bars had been placed "out of bounds" for Canadian soldiers of the Siberian force. (These men were on their way to fight the Bolshevik menace in Vladivostok, Russia. They were part of an international force intended to bring peace to Russia by crushing the "Red Revolution" in its infancy.)

At every turn, the police faced criticism. Even when the culprit was caught red-handed, few charges were laid. For example, during a raid on a "blind pig," the bartender would quickly dump his pitcher of whiskey into a waiting tub of water. When the mixture was tested, if it came to less than 2.5 percent alcohol, there were no penalties. Charges of "offering for sale," were almost always reduced to "possession not in a private dwelling." The deputation blamed departmental sloth and stinginess, claiming that the city of Victoria, in particular, "did not desire to incur the expense of maintaining the prisoners in the provincial jail." City officials immediately pointed out with irritation that alcohol was available in adjacent municipalities, and the city was no softer on drinkers than other areas in the province.

The police also claimed that recent court cases had tied their hands by forcing them to obtain a warrant before making an arrest. But it was hard to obtain the evidence for a search warrant when regular officers were so well known in a community. A "stool pigeon" was required, and this incurred yet more expense and difficulty. Surprisingly, the police at first objected to the use of informers on the grounds that their employment could lead to abuses, such as "the engagement of disreputable characters to assist in entrapping those who have never before sold liquor illegally." It is hard to imagine such niceties being put forth today. The prohibition delegation sneered at these excuses, arguing that stronger enforcement was all that was needed. If the laws already on the books were only applied, it was argued, prohibition would succeed: "the only way to put an end to 'blind-pigging' is to imprison a few of the offenders." It was time to abandon the police's "shilly-shallying methods"; what was needed was a complete "reorganization" of law enforcement. Something had to be done, as everyone, not just the "rabid prohibitionist," was "disgusted with existing conditions." The Reverend Mr. Connell added, "It is becoming intolerable that people year after year must come here and demand enforcement of the law; they keep wondering why they must be taxed to keep up a police force and yet proper enforcement of the law is not secured."[14]

The allure of the fast and easy money to be made selling liquor proved tempting to many. This was perhaps only to be expected, but when the most prominent member of the prohibition camp was found to be involved in smuggling, the credibility of the entire movement took a nosedive. December 1918 saw the eruption of a highly embarrassing scandal that rocked the prohibition movement to its roots and opened the People's Prohibition Association hierarchy to charges of gross hypocrisy. The problem lay with the PPA's choice for Prohibition Commissioner: Walter Chester Findlay, who had been appointed to the post in September 1917 with near-unanimous approval from his friends who ran the organization.

The first news that something was amiss was the announcement on December 11, 1918, that a provincial order-in-council had removed Findlay from office, and the Attorney-General had issued an arrest warrant for importing "a carload of rye whiskey into the province."[15] The very next day, Findlay's car was stopped at Blaine, Washington, by American immigration officials and he was turned back, only to be seized by plainclothes provincial police officers. Although there was no alcohol in the vehicle, an investigation "for some days" had provided incriminating information, and the commissioner was charged with illegal importation of alcohol in breach of the federal order-in-council issued under the War Measures Act. An informant had revealed that Findlay was smuggling in large quantities of alcohol originally intended for legal drugstores or re-export to Mexico. The commissioner was hauled up to Vancouver Provincial Police headquarters, booked, held for twenty-four hours in a comfortable room, and released on $2,000 bail. Visiting friends and PPA members described him as "confident," neither acting nor looking as if he were guilty of the charge. So began a long saga that would cause the prohibitionists endless mortification over the next year.

W.C. Findlay had first appeared on the scene in the summer of 1915, and had soon joined the inner circle of the PPA. Young, personable and ambitious, he proved an able organizer who helped lead the drys to their victory in the September 1916 civilian referendum. He seemed the perfect candidate for Prohibition Commissioner. Interestingly, there was one dissenter to the nomination. John Nelson, owner of the Vancouver *World,* had been a leading member of the PPA since its inception and was now its president. His objection was explained in the Minutes: ". . . it was not because of the suggesting of Mr. W.C. Findlay's name, for he thought he was the very best man in sight, but that he [Nelson] as an editor might feel at perfect liberty to criticize the appointee of the Government if criticism were ever necessary."[16] Whatever Nelson meant by his carefully crafted comment, he had his doubts about the man, and these doubts were soon confirmed.

The magnitude of the charges against Findlay came as a shock to everyone. He was accused of illegally importing 700 cases of high-class Gooterham and Wort rye whiskey into the province with the intent of selling them for personal profit. That amounted to 8,400 bottles — worth $84,000 at ten dollars a bottle, and far more if sold by the drink. This was an enormous sum at a time when a meal in a restaurant cost twenty-five cents, and meat sold for ten cents a pound. There were also unconfirmed reports of many more cases of whiskey missing from the government vendor's store in Vancouver. Findlay pleaded guilty to illegally importing alcohol, and the Magistrate imposed a $1,000 fine, with no jail time and no costs. Passing sentence, he commented laconically ". . . this is a wholesale case of importing into this Province by one in authority. I hereby impose the maximum penalty."[17] Findlay promptly paid his fine and hightailed it on the next boat to Seattle.

The prohibitionists were outraged at this callous betrayal by one of their own. Several members of the PPA, including President John Nelson, called upon the ex-commissioner, begging for an explanation. When it became apparent that Findlay had none, the PPA issued a blistering, unanimous resolution accusing him of "gross fraud and breach of trust." The insignificance of the fine was a further insult.

So much whiskey suggested the existence of a large and sophisticated operation with powerful connections at the highest levels of police and government. If only the ex-commissioner could be compelled to talk, then the whole rotten criminal syndicate could be brought down. But Findlay maintained his silence. All he would tell fellow members of the PPA was that ". . . a year ago when in

Victoria... Tulk had been very active in his attentions on the Commissioner."[18] Once again we see the not-so-subtle hand of A. Edward Tulk in the thick of the anti-prohibition dirty work.

John Oliver, a rustic pig farmer and skilful parliamentarian, had taken over as Liberal Premier in March 1918, after the untimely death of William Brewster. A private meeting was arranged between Findlay and Oliver to give the ex-commissioner a chance to explain himself. Oliver commented afterwards, "I asked him to tell me the whole story so we could get to the bottom of the matter. He absolutely refused to tell me a thing other than admit that he had brought the liquor in as charged.... I desire the Findlay matter probed to the very bottom but I do not know just how this ought to be undertaken."[19] On December 21, the provincial government passed an order-in-council creating the Clement Commission, under Supreme Court Justice Clement to look into the question of illegal importation in general, and the Findlay case in particular. But Findlay proved a most uncooperative witness. Exactly who blew the whistle on Findlay, and why, remains unknown, but such large sums of money brazenly changing hands in this climate of pious hypocrisy infuriated many.

Some prominent members of the government tried to minimize the damage, which did not help matters. Attorney-General Farris actually defended Findlay, claiming that he was a "capable official, in whom I have the utmost confidence."[20] The Board of Police Commissioners, which only a few days earlier had been on the defensive about lackadaisical enforcement, now took the offensive. Several months before, Findlay had made the unfortunate mistake of granting a newspaper interview in which he chastised the police about their indifference to enforcement of the prohibition laws. Now they, in turn, were extremely interested in the source of the ex-commissioner's information, and whether he could prove his statements. Findlay was charged with breach of trust, and subpoenaed to appear before the police board to testify on this and other matters.

But would the disgraced commissioner return from Seattle to testify? He described himself as "down and out" after his arrest and dismissal. When asked if he would appear before the police inquiry, he humbly declined: "I don't see that I can do any good by going up there. I have already written a letter to the Board. I can't get at the books in the department now."[21] There was some talk of warrants and extradition, but it was clear that any prosecution would be long and costly.

After some delay, a deal was worked out between the lawyers; the following week, the disgraced ex-commissioner returned to Victoria. On his return, Liberal Attorney-General Farris did his best to keep Findlay out of jail by quashing the arrest warrant and ordering police "not to touch him."[22] Findlay was offered freedom from prosecution on the theft charge, and leniency on the other charges, as long as he was free and frank in his answers. After grandly promising to tell all, he became reticent on the stand, stating, "I refuse to answer any questions." Findlay was immediately sent to Oakalla prison farm for contempt of court, where he was to wait while the case went forward.[23]

Notwithstanding the apparent loss of its star witness, the police board and Clement Commission unearthed a wealth of information about the inner workings of Findlay's booze bureaucracy. The Prohibition Commissioner had worked in a complete vacuum, with no one to check on his activities. He had hired and fired workers, set up and dismantled liquor warehouses, made deliveries to private homes and businesses — all without files, bookkeeping, or paperwork of any sort. Identifying marks on bottles and boxes were routinely tampered with or removed, and large quantities of liquor would mysteriously vanish from one warehouse, only to reappear in another. Findlay's warehouses at Western Canada Liquor Company Ltd., McGuinness Warehouse and Forwarding Company, Gold Seal Liquor Company Ltd., as well as an unnamed warehouse located at 1114 Hamilton Street — all were at a loss to produce the various manifests, receipts and liquor involved in the charges. Interestingly, Norman Tulk and his brother, the omnipresent A. Edward Tulk, were the co-owners of the Western Canada Liquor Company Ltd.

Without a paper trail, it was obviously impossible to determine what liquor belonged to whom. All that was found in Findlay's office after the arrest were a few invoices and a large pile of blank, but signed, import licences. Exactly what happened to the 700 cases of Gooterham and Wort rye whiskey that had started the fuss in the first place was never determined. Meanwhile the price of illicit liquor in Vancouver took a big leap upward because of a sudden shortage.

Findlay's ingenious lawyers then brought the Clement Commission to a halt by raising the sensitive issue of provincial jurisdiction. They argued that Findlay's testimony before a provincial commission was illegal, because the original charge was a federal violation, which should be heard by a federal body. Muddling the issue of Findlay's criminal activities with the tedious question of provincial versus federal jurisdiction was a brilliant act of jurisprudence. His lawyers petitioned the provincial Supreme Court to grant an aptly named "writ of prohibition." When the Court agreed, Findlay was released from prison.

The Conservative opposition had a field day. Bowser crowed that Liberal Attorney-General Farris had been working hand in glove with Findlay all along:

> Findlay walked the streets of Victoria notwithstanding the fact that the Attorney-General had knowledge of his rascality. Then he went to Vancouver where he stayed a little too long and was captured at the boundary whither he had been driven by one of the whisky dealers of Vancouver. It was strange that Findlay's counsel had been a close political friend of the Attorney-General . . . [and] . . . that the simplest charge against him that could be brought was laid and that after having been fined Findlay calmly left for Seattle via Victoria and under the very nose of the Attorney-General. . . . Apparently there was another justice for the man who dealt in liquor, not by the bottle or drink, but by the carload.[24]

The ex-commissioner remained free for several months, but his crookedness and uncanny ability to avoid testifying on the stand had made him many enemies. Most of the charges against him were eventually dropped for lack of evidence, but he was finally convicted and sentenced to two years imprisonment for the vague charges of breach of trust and "scandalous abuse of his position."[25]

It is clear that W.C. Findlay was handled with kid gloves from the beginning. He received special treatment from the government and police at every stage of the scandal. To his credit — or discredit — he never talked, despite frequent promises to bare all. This is not surprising, for with such lenient treatment there was really no reason to expose the inner workings of this vastly profitable criminal enterprise. Certainly the reluctance of the authorities to prosecute him suggests their own involvement at the highest levels. Members in the House routinely held Findlay up as an example of the wave of prohibition corruption sweeping the province, but there seemed little desire to force him to testify. Findlay took the rap and did his two years, while the big fish remained untouched. He was undoubtedly amply rewarded when released.

In March a second scandal broke, which, though not nearly as serious as the Findlay affair, was still highly embarrassing for the prohibitionists. Police Commissioner M.B. Martinson from North Vancouver, head of the prohibition movement on the North Shore and long-time member of the PPA executive, had just arrived at a Methodist anniversary social. He was met there by North Vancouver Mayor Vance and a policeman, and asked to return home for a search of his house on Lonsdale Avenue. Based on a tip they had received, police conducted a house search without a warrant, and "a jar of liquor, apparently whiskey" was discovered in a coal bin beneath the kitchen. Because he used his home as an office, it did not constitute a "dwelling" in which liquor could be legally held by the owner. Martinson angrily protested that the booze was a "plant" claiming that he had just been in the basement to feed the coal stove and it was "certainly not present at that time." He also claimed to be a total abstainer who had not touched a drop in eighteen years. One of the constables noticed a suspicious leaf adhering to the jug, which suggested that it had indeed recently been brought in from outside.

Like Findlay, Martinson had been loud and careless in making charges about weak police enforcement of prohibition. North Vancouver's Chief of Police, Arthur Davies, had been forced to resign because of these allegations. Now Davies struck back by providing evidence to investigators of whiskey deliveries made to the Lonsdale address and signed for by Martinson. The ensuing court case generated wide interest, and featured a dramatic debate between the counsel and bench over whether "prohibition created hypocrisy." The North Vancouver police commissioner was found guilty of possession in what came to be called "the little brown jug incident." He immediately appealed. In granting the appeal, Judge More commented, "From the evidence that has been given before me, I have no hesitation in saying that in my judgement Mr. Martinson was just as innocent of having that jar of liquor placed in his cellar as I was...."[26] More and more, it began to appear to the public that the loudest boosters of prohibition were the biggest hypocrites. And, most disturbing of all, this scandal reinforced the view that there was a double standard of justice in the province — one for the well connected, and another for the common folk.

In fact, the provincial legal structure was at a serious disadvantage when it came to prosecuting Findlay and others. The grandly named Prohibition Commissioner, who administered the Act, had no police powers of search, seizure or law enforcement. His main role was to coordinate and administer the sale of liquor to government vendors, who in turn provided it to legitimate doctors, druggists, clergy and industry. He also listened sympathetically to complaints of liquor violations, and passed the information on to the authorities.

Money for enforcement was another problem, as the province provided little. Similarly, municipalities, having given up the taxes and liquor licence money, were forced to pay police from other meagre revenues. Even confiscated liquor was turned over to the province for resale by government vendors, with none of the proceeds going to the municipalities involved in the seizure. Further, as was indicated earlier, the number and quality of constables declined during the war, as many volunteered for the trenches.

Federal-provincial turf disputes further muddied the waters. Real enforcement, with hundreds of officers and large prisons, was simply impossible with the resources available. With so much to do and so little with which to do it, investigations were inevitably bogged down.

There was also growing evidence that liquor prohibition would not solve society's many problems. When one intoxicant was removed from society, people tended to replace it with something else — often with something that could be even more dangerous to the user. A story in the *Daily Colonist*, reprinted from the *London Daily Mail*, breathlessly warned of the dangers of other drugs, such as cocaine, opium, morphine and heroin:

> The craving and its consequences are much more terrible in the case of drugs than in alcoholic patients. . . . During the last two years, and especially during the last six months, we have had very many patients who were confirmed drug victims and the list is growing daily. . . . Before 1914 drug-taking was confined to the ultra-artistic sect and a few of the leisured classes, but with the arrival of Colonial and American contingents the habit spread until it became a cult.[27]

Police Commissioner Buckworth alleged that there was "an international ring, controlling the sale, importation and manufacture of these narcotics with shrewd white men at the head of it, some of whom are criminals of the worst kind. . . . The Chinese [he claimed] hold out inducements to their young customers by saying, 'You get me customer, me give you drug heap cheap yourself.'"[28]

The allure of illegal narcotics seemed to recede after January 1920 when the Dominion order-in-council expired (although narcotics remained popular in Chinese communities throughout North America). Alcohol could once again be imported from out-of-province, and warehouses were immediately swamped with liquor orders. The loosening of the law apparently stirred the entrepreneurial spirit of many, while exciting the ire of prohibitionists. Thirty-eight export liquor warehouses promptly opened in the province under close police supervision.[29] Sister warehouses were set up just over the border in Alberta to facilitate easy and legal shipment by Dominion Express. Transportation companies were suddenly overwhelmed with orders, and deliveries in Vancouver continued both day and night. Department stores started selling liquor by mail order, and express companies had to build special warehouses to supply the booming trade. Some private cellars reputedly contained up to $40,000 worth of liquor — which was seen as a bit excessive for even the most devoted dipsomaniac.

Many enterprising bootleggers began to produce their own hooch in quantity. According to the PPA, the police had shut down more than 121 large stills by March 1920. Like some of today's marijuana "grow-operations," many of the distilling operations involved extensive home renovations and were highly sophisticated.[30] In the spring of 1919, an 80-gallon still was discovered hidden in the attic of a home in Vancouver. The floor joists had been strengthened to take the extra weight, and zinc sheeting had been laid down to prevent leaks. A trapdoor in the bedroom closet provided access.

In one month alone, the Vancouver dry squad raided 108 bootleg joints and eighteen disorderly houses, collecting $9,750 in fines. It was no different in the rest of Canada. In 1917, some 191 stills were discovered and destroyed. In 1920, there were 985; and by 1923, the number rose to 1,100 stills.

A number of ingenious schemes were hatched in 1919 to help replace the large liquid shortfall created by the Findlay affair. On May 9, eight "huge" cases of "electrical goods" en route from Montreal to a local company were seized by police and found to contain forty cases of rye whiskey.[31] Three weeks later, one and one-quarter tons of "ink" from the Dominion Ink Company of Montreal was intercepted on its way to the BC Ink and Roller Company of Vancouver. "It was very peculiar ink. That was why it roused curiosity. The whole ton and a quarter was of a light amber color, and was contained in quart bottles with gold labels on, packed a dozen to the case. The labels proclaimed the ink to be of the 'G and W' variety. The stuff looked, smelled and tasted more like rye than ink." In fact it was whiskey. The editor of the *Victoria Daily Times* commented:

> It is a matter of surprise that some energetic and enterprising public official has not risen to the occasion and invented a sort of pocket X-ray apparatus for issuance to municipal and provincial policemen. Some such innovation will be necessary if the inventive faculties of eastern shippers of 'wet' goods continue to develop at the present rate of progress. . . . The Eastern shipper's repertoire of camouflage must be fairly well exhausted by this time. Chewing gum, ink, paint, feeding bottles, and talcum powder have failed. Hair-oil, however, is yet to be heard from.[32]

A complex distribution system evolved, with the rich taking regular deliveries of bonded liquor from uniformed liverymen, while the poor made their buys on the street. Sikhs marketed whiskey out of their turbans in Vancouver, and trucks loaded with "embalming fluid" sold to do-it-yourself funeral home operators.

On the streets of the province one could find all manner of alcoholic beverages for sale, but bureaucratic officialdom tended to be extremely stuffy about bending the rules. In a letter marked "Confidential," the Provincial Secretary asked Attorney-General Farris about providing wine and spirits for the recently appointed Lieutenant-Governor Admiral Jellicoe and his entourage, then in Victoria. The men were unused to the strictures of prohibition, and had made a special request for several cases of Madeira, sherry, champagne, "best scotch," "best brandy" and "6 bottles of Italian vermouth or Orange bitters" for a party at Government House. Farris would have none of it, and responded testily in a confidential memorandum:

> My Dear Doctor:
> I see no reason why his Honor the Lieutenant-Governor should not conform to the law as well as anyone else, and so far as I am concerned, I must absolutely decline to accede to the request.[33]

But the farce of prohibition in British Columbia had run its course. Bribes and payoffs for special treatment had become a part of daily life. Corruption and scandal had reached into the very heart of the prohibition camp. The police and politicians could no longer be relied upon to enforce the law. Speakeasies and "blind pigs" operated in Vancouver, Victoria and smaller towns with impunity. An enormous bootlegging industry had sprung up overnight to satisfy the unquenchable craving. Soldiers returning from the front were particularly incensed.

The unions had never supported the law, and the business community felt alienated by the unfulfilled promise of compensation. After many delays and false starts, Premier John Oliver appointed a Royal Commission to investigate the issue in 1919. In January 1920, Justice Morrison ruled that compensation applied only to physical property that had been expropriated by the government. Thus valuable licences and businesses sacrificed to improve the general welfare of the public did not require compensation. The collapse of the compensation issue created a sense of betrayal in the business community that was not soon forgotten.

After the initial celebrations at the war's end, there was little cheer or prosperity in British Columbia. The spirit of idealism and unity engendered by the struggle had been replaced by a profound disillusionment, for the enormous sacrifices had brought little gain for most. Economic and social dislocation followed the much-vaunted Armistice, as the country and province tried desperately to return to some measure of normalcy. Within days of peace, contracts were cancelled, factories put up for sale, and thousands of workers laid off. Labour unrest had intensified in the last years of the war, with strikes at the Crowsnest coal fields, the Trail smelter, and among longshoremen, shipyard workers and metal workers in the province. Record numbers of workers walked off the job in the first Canadian general strike in August 1918. With the formation of One Big Union in March 1919, Conservatives and Liberals alike viewed the rising labour unrest with horror. Oliver blamed "a handful of agitators" throughout Canada who were attempting to overthrow constitutional government and substitute it with a "dictatorship." He said, "I am convinced that the Bolshevists are behind all this turmoil."[34]

▲ The Vancouver Dry Squad proudly displaying confiscated stills and liquor, c. 1918. (COURTESY CITY OF VANCOUVER ARCHIVES, CVA 480-215)

▶ A Victoria City Policeman stands "at the ready" next to his "paddy wagon," 1 August 1918. (COURTESY CITY OF VICTORIA ARCHIVES, PR131-598)

▲ The BC Provincial Police lived in the communities they policed and were not issued uniforms until 1924. BCPP group at Prince George, c. 1918. (COURTESY BC ARCHIVES, A-08431)

▲ The Vancouver Dry Squad was noted for its diligence in combating the liquor menace. Depicted here in 1921 are (from top left) Jim Copland, A. Gibb, Gordon Ward, Jos. B. Riley, Currie, (and bottom left) Sutherland and Charles Tulley.
(COURTESY CITY OF VANCOUVER ARCHIVES, CVA480-120)

▶ The small municipal police force of Burnaby saw no need for a Dry Squad, c. 1921.
(COURTESY BC ARCHIVES, A-08093)

Oliver proved to be an honest but weak leader. He appointed a number of commissions to investigate the railroad bond fiasco and election fraud, and fired hundreds of civil servants installed by the Conservatives. But the economy remained in the doldrums, and the Liberals seemed powerless to do anything about it. Ironically, the post-war depression gave a tremendous boost to the province's moonshine producers. Alcohol production became one of the most reliable survival strategies for British Columbians in the early twenties and it primed the taps for the huge expansion in rum-running to America that would soon take place.

As the economic crises deepened, banks called in their loans and raised interest rates to curb inflation. British Columbia's debt, including railway bond guarantees, had reached a crippling $85 million. The thousands of returning soldiers faced falling wages, 25 percent unemployment, and conflict with militant workers — along with their own physical and mental scars. The provincial government had promised the returning veterans loans, land, civil service jobs, liquor reform, and other support, but it never seemed to materialize. The idea of the Social Gospel had lost much of its resonance by 1919. Men and women no longer felt they could shape their destiny by tinkering with the social and political fabric. The world had become a great deal more complicated. Yet the war had been brought to a successful conclusion, and the hated "Hun" vanquished. On the supply front, once again, grains and sugar were cheap and plentiful. How long would the public be willing to accept the strictures of prohibition?

CHAPTER 9

THE TRIUMPH OF MODERATION

AT THE END OF THE war, the province faced recession and a crushing provincial debt of $21 million, plus an additional $64 million in railroad bond guarantees. These obligations were created when the McBride government rashly offered to guarantee railroad company bonds for upwards of $35,000 a mile at 4 percent over thirty years. When the schemes proved a failure, Victoria was left holding the debt. There was no longer any provincial income for the sale of forest and agricultural land, since McBride had already sold everything of value years before. Some means of generating revenue had to be found. The federal government had already brought in a number of new and creative taxes to pay for the war, including the first business tax in 1916 and personal income tax in 1917. There was even talk of a 1 percent provincial tax on all incomes in Vancouver and an increase in property taxes for home improvements. One of the most intriguing suggestions for obtaining plentiful tax revenues was to re-legalize booze.

The liquor industry had once employed thousands and had provided valuable tax and licensing revenues. Now, criminal bootleggers were pocketing that money — and they paid taxes to no one. Many pointed to Quebec, which had had a prohibition law permitting sale of beer and wine since April 1919. That province was now doing a booming business serving thirsty refugees from the rest of Canada and the United States. A Quebec tax study demonstrated that if municipalities were allowed to keep 50 percent of the profits from the legal sale of liquor, their financial problems would vanish. As public support evaporated, questions began to be raised about what should replace prohibition. All agreed that there could be no return to the riotous open bar. Perhaps a middle way could be found that allowed for moderate drinking in private — but only under strict conditions, which would, of course, include a sizeable revenue tax.

The Findlay fiasco in January 1919 accelerated the search for alternatives. Disgusted citizens in Vancouver launched a movement under the name of the People's Moderation Party (PMP) to bring together the many opponents of prohibition. "Influential men and women in British Columbia, including doctors, lawyers, returned soldiers, labourers and artisans, merchants, and financiers" were invited to join. Business celebrities such as Aitken Tweedale, Charles H. Tupper, E.H. Beazley, Henry Bell-Irving, and Dr. D.J. O'Neil were in the forefront of a skilful publicity campaign, first in the two major cities, and later throughout the province. The new group was quick to reassure the public that there would be no return to the days of unrestricted drinking. Mr. Tweedale told the press:

> The main issue of the People's Moderation Party is based upon British fair play. We ask for amendments to present legislation that will permit the sale of what is known as 'hard liquor' under Government supervision to all persons within reasonable limits and the sale too of light beers and wines. We are strongly against any move to re-establish the system of bars as they had existed.[1]

And he emphasized that prohibition in its present form was "most unfair and un-British." Declaring itself "non-political and non-sectarian," the group took pains to distance itself from the liquor industry, being well aware of the danger of being smeared as a tool of the whiskey barons. Light wine and beer should be allowed with restaurant meals, and spirits provided in closed packages from government liquor stores. Other moderation and "liberty league" groups soon sprouted up around the province. In mid-March, Premier John Oliver received a deputation of Moderation Party members who called for yet another vote on the liquor issue.

He listened carefully and was heard to observe: "I have never been drunk in my life and am no friend of the liquor traffic, but I have lived long enough to know that prohibition cannot be enforced in British Columbia in the present state of public feeling."[2] John W. Farris, Oliver's Attorney-General, agreed, reminding British Columbians of the narrowness of the prohibition vote in 1917. He noted that many had seen prohibition as a temporary war measure, which should be reconsidered now that the troops were safely home. If the act were truly unworkable, it should be reexamined, and perhaps even abandoned. But a half-baked enforcement policy was the worst option of all: "Prohibition, which does not prohibit, is worse than useless and contempt for law, persisted in openly, will undermine a people's morals just as surely as will alcohol or any other pernicious drugs."[3]

In April 1920, Farris announced that there would indeed be another referendum, and for the first time both sexes would vote. But the wording of the ballot was disturbingly vague and non-binding:

Which do you prefer?
(a) The present Prohibition Act, or
(b) An act to provide for the government control and sale in sealed packages of spirituous and malt liquors?

In spite of the weak language of the ballot, it was clear that the Liberals were distancing themselves from prohibition, one of their most sacred policies for over a decade. Yet Farris also argued against a return to public drinking in hotels and saloons, claiming such a policy would "cloud" the issue. He was also unwilling to consider a referendum on importation of liquor into British Columbia after the 1920 expiry of the Dominion order-in-council. The question was, how much longer would the Liberals be able to maintain this difficult juggling act?

In Ottawa, the Dominion Government was also coming under pressure to loosen up. In February a large deputation of labour union members arrived in the capital, demanding real beer for the workers. Resolutions from 1,500 of the 1,700 existing unions in Canada were presented, and workers argued that these numbers proved that "the active minority who are preaching total prohibition do not represent the thoughts and desires of the great masses of workers of this country." Furthermore, they maintained that the 1918 order-in-council banning liquor was intended as a "war measure" and not a piece of "social legislation." The war was now over and there was "no further need of this measure of restriction, if ever such need existed." The workers also warned that if more and stronger beer were not provided in Canada, potential English immigrants would head elsewhere. They argued that "if Canada is to attract British Immigration instead of the unsatisfactory alien immigration of the past, the laws of the Dominion must be such as commend themselves to possible immigrants."[4]

British Columbia's returned veterans also made their case when a delegation of soldiers arrived in Victoria and presented Oliver with an anti-prohibition petition bearing 33,000 signatures. Significantly, another pro-moderation petition signed by 8,000 women suggested that their votes in favour of prohibition could no longer be counted on. The People's Prohibition Association had suffered a precipitous drop in popularity, and a note of desperation began to creep into its pronouncements. As a show of strength, more than 500 cheering delegates (down from 4,000 in 1915) attended a convention held at St. Andrew's Church in Vancouver. While numbers had obviously decreased, the *World* continued to report optimistically that "in numbers, enthusiasm, vigour of utterance and aggressive fighting spirit it eclipsed any gathering yet held."[5] A slate of new officers was elected, in most cases unanimously, there were renewed demands that Findlay be compelled to testify under oath, a recommended $10,000 budget was endorsed, and the notion that there should be Canada-wide prohibition received wholehearted support.

The redoubtable Nellie McClung made another appearance, but she lacked the fervour and fire of her 1915 convention success. Now she admitted that "prohibition prohibits but does not annihilate," but she still contended that prohibition was better than the government putting "its seal on the liquor business." And when she concluded that, "if you allow the sale of liquor, you will have to take the responsibility as you will be in partnership with the traffic," it sounded almost as if she knew her cause were losing strength.[6] And, as an indication of how public opinion had changed, McClung received a threatening phone call just before her presentation at the Orpheum.

Although the prohibitionists appeared to be losing ground, the hard core PPA was not yet willing to surrender to the wets. If the police were unwilling to enforce the law, the prohibitionists would fill that function themselves. Over the years the organization had become much more centralized. Members met much less frequently, and paid staff had replaced volunteers. The day-to-day work of fundraising, dissemination of propaganda and investigation fell into the capable hands of Reverend W.G. Fortune, the executive secretary. The scandals had brought about many significant changes in the prohibition bureaucracy. Most importantly, the responsibility for purchasing and managing government liquor stocks had been transferred directly to the Attorney-General's office, allowing the commissioner to concentrate his efforts on enforcement. But with neither funding nor police powers, his efforts could do little.

With these changes, the main thrust of the PPA shifted away from founding a liquor-free Zion to hardscrabble criminal investigation. In a bizarre turn of events, this civic group became an enthusiastic arm of the law. Private detectives were hired, and loyal citizens were called upon to become snitches. People were encouraged to conduct their own investigations and report their findings directly to the PPA, which relayed the information to the Prohibition Commissioner. In this way, a covert spy network was organized to scout out and report on violators. The letter files of the PPA began to look more like the earlier files of the Provincial Police. In February 1918, Reverend Fortune received the following chummy letter concerning the wide-open border trade in Surrey:

> I proposed to call on my friend, the Surrey Chief of police, and see if we could not put a stop to the traffic and I was advised by those *who claim to know*, not to do anything of the kind, as poor Alex was as deep in the mire as any of the others. (I might state this was a bitter disappointment to me) and worse I am further informed that the *Customs men* on *both* sides of the line know of the business, needless for me to state, I can scarcely believe this report.... Hence I came to the conclusion, the better way to deal with the matter would be to have a stranger sent out here who had discretion and common sense who could round up the parties, who are responsible for the traffic, so as not to incriminate the officials for the *credit of our country*. I can but feel for some of them, if they are guilty. As for the others we know their record.
>
> Yours Truly, Henry Thrift[7]

From Rosedale the word reached Fortune that someone was tipping off the locals to any attempted enforcement. Some good advice was also offered:

> I fear the whiskey ring have a spy on you for each time you send a detective up here he is announced before he arrives.... I mention these things to let you know how it goes. I think the kind of detectives we need is a lumber jack looking over the country or a traveling agent, or teacher, anything so long as he is a good mixer and gets in with the worst classes, gets samples of the stuff that is to be found. I don't think that these fellows with the silver star and red braid are much good on the job.[8]

Fortune passed much of this information to the newly appointed Prohibition Commissioner, Colonel J. Sclater, who had replaced Findlay. Unlike his predecessor, Sclater was an honest man who came to have serious doubts about the viability of post-war prohibition. He sounded a strong note of moderation when dealing with the puritanical PPA. When Fortune berated him over 6-percent beer openly being sold at the Eating House and Ark Hotel in Port Alberni, he responded: "It is not a matter for great surprise that drunkenness is rife at Alberni when liquor can be imported into the Province by any private individual who cares to do so in any quantity he pleases. Drunkenness is, I am sorry to say, not confined to Alberni and so long as the present Act remains in effect I do not see how drunkenness is to be prevented."[9] Despite Sclater's own doubts, there was no shortage of those who enthusiastically stepped forward to become travelling informants, and for a time a climate of paranoia prevailed, with thirsty strangers everywhere being treated with suspicion.

Reverend Fortune himself continued to write to Sclater, pleading for greater financial support for his informants and arguing that victory was just around the corner:

> Some time ago you stated in our office that if men could secure convictions you were willing to pay for it and pay well. I mentioned the fact that a couple of fellows were taking a trip through the Kamloops district. One was in to see me a few minutes ago. He reported that they secured evidence against Mrs. Sally who got 12 months for selling liquor. Agent Brown for gambling, $100 fine, while an Italian skipped against whom they had evidence for gambling and selling liquor.
>
> They are out of pocket on the trip and of course have nothing for their work.... They are talking of leaving the city if not given employment.... They say they can make a clean up of this city if given a chance at all. They may leave Tuesday hence the rush,
>
> Yours Sincerely, Reverend Fortune[10]

The delusions of the PPA reached their height in February 1920, when a delegation of fifty members held a meeting with Oliver and urged a complete reorganization of prohibition enforcement in the province. All present administrators of the Act would be sacked, and replaced by three independent commissioners endowed with special powers. Ominously, the new administrators were to be "removed from the ordinary machinery of government with a board of outstanding citizens in charge, controlling their own legal and police machinery." These conditions, of course, would create the trappings of a classic police state. A separate court system and police force having no oversight from government sounded more like something from Leninist Russia than British Columbia. In effect, such heavy-handed suggestions placed the PPA beyond the pale for both the Conservatives and the Liberals, who were not willing to turn society upside down in a final massive effort to eradicate booze.

Attorney-General Farris frostily rejected the recommendation, commenting that although he might be glad to "shoulder the responsibility off on someone else," he did not like "the imputation that it should be taken from the attorney-general and given to someone else who could look after it." Farris took time to complain that he had been the victim of "more cruel and unfair allegations in connection with the enforcement of the Prohibition Act than with all other things put together." The Attorney-General was also cool about a suggestion that would place the possession limit in the home at two quarts of hard liquor and two gallons of malted beer. He pointed out that this would run counter to the fundamental principle that a Briton's home is his castle, and also that enforcement in the home would present "problems."[11] Increasingly, the privacy issue was coming to the fore. If prohibition meant posting a guard in every household, the price in liberty and privacy would be too much to bear.

After offering their extreme solution, the prohibitionists began to lose credibility in Victoria, and the Moderation Party's position was significantly strengthened. Oliver dithered, but everyone knew that another vote was inevitable. Finally, on September 10, 1920, a plebiscite was scheduled for October 10. The Premier, who had supported prohibition in 1916, remained personally non-committal to the end. On the eve of the vote, he commented vaguely, "I consider the vote as one that liquor shall be on sale in reasonable quantities at a reasonable price, and not be abused. I have no conscientious scruples about making all I can out of the business."[12]

In contrast to the original referendum in 1916, the 1920 campaign was virtually devoid of the earlier melodrama and religious moralizing. There was little heckling, and only mild interest among most. One heard the usual accusations of corruption, with prominent government officials allegedly being for sale, and bootleggers delivering money to politicians in paper bags. Some tried to tie illegal liquor to drug smuggling, "white slavery" and Asian immigration. On the whole, however, both the politicians and the voters seemed apathetic. Predictably, the drys brought up their old conspiracy bugaboo, blaming the liquor barons, brewers, hotel owners, distilleries and even the wine industry of France. To most British Columbians, it was the same tired old line that they had heard too many times before.

The Moderation Party and its smaller sibling, the Liberty League, hammered away on one indisputable fact: prohibition was unenforceable in British Columbia. The view that alcohol was the root cause of all of society's problems no longer held sway; a more complex and worldly attitude had taken its place. Booze had now come to be seen as just one among many social problems — more a symptom than a root cause of bad behaviour.

Some new and very effective appeals began to appear in letters to the newspapers. H. Hastings of Victoria blasted the darker aspects of British Columbia's prohibition. The web of secrecy, subterfuge, informants and lies which had sprung up so quickly seemed a heavy price to pay for this booze-less utopia. Listing the advantages of controlled liquor sales in government stores, the writer observed in part that

- It will stop the turning of private houses into secret stills, to the detriment of the children, who knowing that it is against the law and seeing their parents do it, have, since Prohibition came into effect, on many occasions under my own limited notice, stolen some to see what it is like, and 'oh mother makes such a good dandelion wine, I took some and it went to my head and it felt so funny.' This will be stopped.

- There will not be a large army of demoralizing spies and stool-pigeons. It will not be necessary for the normal man, who is a moderate drinker, to flout the law in contempt, or to lower his moral standards to evade a law which he feels is a distinct encroachment upon his inalienable rights and liberty, which has been handed down to him from the time of King John.

- Doctors will regain their conscience. The poor man who has not the money to have his liquor will be able to get what he wants without the demoralizing pretence of illness and paying of his hard-earned wages for prescriptions. . . . Since the government will sell only at a moderate profit, no one will pay a high enough price at the bootleggers and saloons (since he can get what he wants at much less cost) and, therefore, the profits which bootleggers can make will not be commensurate with the risks he runs. This will very materially reduce the incentive to bootlegging. It is the big profits under Prohibition which is the incentive for bootlegging.[13]

By contrast, the advertisements of the drys took on a peevish and tepid quality stressing the negative while offering no new ideas on how to make their noble moral experiment work better:

"THEY SAY" The Wet Moderates and the Moderate Wets have one cure for everything. It is — "MORE BOOZE"
They Say that drunkenness has increased. Their cure — ,
  MORE BOOZE
They Say that the drug habit has increased. Their cure — ,
  MORE BOOZE
They Say there is a huge increase in crime. Their cure — ,
  MORE BOOZE
They Say we are becoming a nation of bootleggers. Their cure,
  MORE BOOZE
They Say prohibition destroys personal liberty — revive it with
  MORE BOOZE.
They Say Government Sale will solve the tax question. How?
  by selling MORE BOOZE

> They Say the worker is becoming discontented — Souse him with
> MORE BOOZE
> THIS MEANS A DELUGE OF BOOZE!
> DON'T BE FOOLED — VOTE FOR PROHIBITION![14]

The drys proceeded to speak loftily of the "only feasible plan to stop Bootlegging" without ever explaining what exactly that entailed — other than more of the same. They noted that prohibition had really been a "blessing," reducing crime and improving health, and that government control would mean government "boozeoriums" outside schools, churches and homes, with deadly results. Frequent public rallies and door-to-door canvassing were organized to drum up public interest, and 85,000 copies of the *Prohibition Bulletin* were handed out.

The PPA expended more money and effort than the wets, and received strong support from the *World*. Even so, the prohibitionists found it impossible to raise the kind of money that had poured so readily into their collection bowls in 1916. Every town and district was assessed a certain amount, and then the local committee would try to raise that amount: $16,000 for Vancouver, $650 for Nanaimo, $600 for Penticton, and so on. Eventually even Fortune complained to a business supporter, "I am free to admit that it [is] more difficult to raise funds under the present circumstances than ever in the past. So many seemed carried away with the thought of Government Control."[15] By the completion of the plebiscite the PPA had spent more than $30,000 and found themselves $9,000 in debt.

The Moderation Party held informal meetings in school basements and civic centers, while the drys favoured mass meetings in large rented halls and auditoriums. Although the Moderationists were again depending on the labour vote, not all workers were against prohibition. Drink might provide needed jobs and comforting solace after a hard day's work, but it also kept the worker docile and complacent. The waves of labour unrest after the war had left some workers so angry that a number were willing to forego their precious beer to keep the union strong. R.P. Pettipiece, the well-known socialist, was against prohibition in 1917, but voted for it in 1920. He argued: "The wage slave that tries to drown the misery of daily toil and poverty in 'booze' is hopeless. He can be neither organized nor educated and it will require a sober, organized and educated working class to emancipate itself from wage slavery."[16] One hears in this reasoning a new twist on Marx's "the opiate of the people."

Another reason for the alienation of some workers was that the Moderationists included in their leadership some of the most prominent capitalists and businessmen in the province. During a Moderation rally, a Commander Reid unwisely argued that prohibition was bad for society because it kept the workers sober and made them aware of their difficulties in the work place: "Reds and revolutionaries were being made of formerly quiet workers who now found time to dwell upon troubles, real and imaginary, and who are becoming sulky and grouchy." Indignant workers responded with an ad in the *BC Federationist:* "Keep the Worker Soused. SOME Compliment to Labour! VOTE FOR PROHIBITION."[17]

Both sides confidently predicted a win, but the Moderationists truly smelled victory. By the end of the campaign, their main concern was that voter apathy would allow the well-organized prohibitionists to triumph yet again. "Just get the voters out to cast their ballot" became their rallying cry. The following little "poem" appeared in the *Sun*, urging all citizens to do their duty by voting:

>APATHY
>The Greatest Enemy of Freedom
>Whether you are a Prohibitionist or for
>Moderation and Government Control, do your
>Duty by British-Columbia and
>VOTE.[18]

On October 20, 1920, the plebiscite was held, and the results surprised everyone. The vote *for* government sale and *against* prohibition was 92,095 while only 55,448 were in favour of continuing the ban on drinking. After the close "win" of four years before, prohibition had now been decisively rejected by a majority of almost 40,000 out of over 147,000 voters. Despite the Moderationist's own predictions, Victoria and Vancouver went overwhelmingly wet. In fact, only Chilliwack and Richmond produced a majority for continued prohibition, although the vote was close in many areas such as Grand Forks, Nelson, the South Okanagan and Slocan.

SAMPLE RETURNS	GOV'T CONTROL	PROHIBITION
South Vancouver	5156	2988
North Vancouver	1430	805
Richmond	2730	2965
Kamloops	905	618
Trail	690	375
Fernie	613	236
Ashcroft	129	46
Nelson	891	914
Victoria	9286	5091
Cowichan	1820	731
Nanaimo	1960	864[19]

The unexpected lopsidedness of the vote stunned Premier Oliver. In a statement to the *World*, he responded defensively:

> I am very much surprised at the result of the vote yesterday — I had anticipated a majority for prohibition. The government will be prepared to submit for the consideration of the legislature a bill to give effect to the will of the people as expressed at the polls. Had the government not been prepared to accept the decision of the electors, they would not have submitted the question. The sweeping majority in favour of government control is ample justification of the government's conduct, both as to the form of the question and the expense of submitting it apart from any other question.[20]

He refused, however to interpret the result as a return to the bar and the saloon, but decided that the vote meant that liquor should be available in "reasonable quantities."

Reverend Fortune, on the other hand, immediately began casting around for an explanation for the defeat of prohibition, and soon found the perfect scapegoat. It was "the immaturity of girl voters without sufficient age and experience to judge the problems of life." For good measure he added a second explanation — "the apathy on the part of a great number of persons." He claimed that he felt certain that within a short time there will be a desire on the part of the public "to undo what they have done today." Mixing his metaphors, he charged that the electors had "created a stew in which they must sizzle for a time."[21] Dr. George Telford, ex-president of the prohibition movement, agreed with Fortune. He blamed the rout on the "failure of women to support us with their votes, the discrediting of the act by lax enforcement, and the psychological effect of the two words moderation and control." He stoutly maintained that they were "not discouraged" and that they would sit back and see with great interest "what sort of bill the Moderationists will bring forward."[22]

Women, newly enfranchised, had been expected to vote solidly dry, but had in fact deserted the cause in droves. The old alliances between the prohibitionists and Liberals, the prohibitionists and women had been torn asunder once and for all. Idealistic optimism about a future free from alcohol had been replaced by an acceptance that this goal was unrealistic and even destructive to society. With support from neither the Conservatives nor the Liberals, prohibition was clearly doomed.

CHAPTER 10

THE LIQUOR CONTROL BOARD AND A NEW KIND OF BAR

FOLLOWING THE DRAMATIC defeat of the prohibition plebiscite, Attorney-General Farris urged Oliver to capitalize on the victory and hold a new provincial election. Within days the Premier complied, and the date was set for December 1, 1920. This turned out to be a serious miscalculation on the part of the Liberals. Public anger over the economy, labour unrest, jobless veterans and the corruption on both sides of the house had led to widespread dissatisfaction with the government. While Oliver thought he could easily defeat the discredited Conservative leader Billy Bowser, he had not reckoned on a host of new contenders. There were now 153 candidates vying for 47 seats, with dozens of new fringe parties such as the Women's Freedom League, the Independent Socialists and the Independent Farmers. When all the votes were counted, the Liberals were returned, but with a much-diminished majority

— twenty-four seats out of forty-seven. Fifteen seats went to the Conservatives, three to the Independents and four to Labour.

Oliver found himself politically weakened and dependent on a wavering coalition. At the same time, however, the election breathed fresh life into the House, bringing many new faces into Victoria. Moreover, the legislature no longer split entirely down party lines: wets and drys, veterans and women could be found on the same ticket for many parties. Unfortunately this disparity of views also made it difficult to agree about anything, and the legislature soon became deadlocked on several crucial issues.

All agreed, however, that the plebiscite vote must be respected, and liquor made available to the public in government outlets. It fell to Premier Oliver to oversee the task of organizing a retail liquor monopoly from the ground up, and quickly. When it was announced that liquor stores were slated to open on June 15, 1921, the province had to scramble to meet the opening deadline. The government had little idea and no experience of how to set up a system of provincial liquor outlets — a business normally controlled by the private sector. There were precedents, however. Scandinavia had experimented with the Gothenburg system, in which a municipality operated non-profit retail liquor outlets under tight regulation. South Carolina had set up state liquor stores between 1893 and 1907, and Saskatchewan had instituted government "dispensaries" in 1915. Quebec adopted government sales, without a vote, in 1921 just weeks before British Columbia opened its stores.

British Columbia's Government Liquor Act, or Moderation Act, as it came to be called, was introduced in the British Columbia legislature in February, and passed the next month. Government stores would sell liquor and beer in sealed packages for a uniform price throughout the province, but buying booze would now be much more difficult than it was in 1917. The new outlets, aptly nicknamed "John Oliver's Drugstores," were highly regulated: authorities would keep a close eye on patrons both on and off store premises. An annual five-dollar permit was required for purchase at the liquor outlets, a permit that would be provided only after a character check. Permits were scrutinized and stamped after each purchase, and at first there was a limit to these cash-and-carry transactions: twelve bottles of full strength beer.

The new law placed a heavy emphasis on law enforcement. Provincial authorities could search a home without a warrant and could confiscate liquor if they suspected that it had been obtained illegally. Anyone caught with unauthorized bottles could be charged with bootlegging and sentenced to six months of hard labour without option of a fine. Unruly drinkers who caused trouble to themselves, their families or society could be "interdicted" until further notice, and lose their permits. Near-beer, fondly referred to as "beaver or ferret's piss," was banished. Public drunkenness, previously a federal crime, now also became a provincial one, along with a ban on "drinking in public." Even inebriation in private was forbidden, punishable by a $100 fine or sixty days, although how this would be enforced was open to question. Liquor Control Board workers who were caught imbibing on the job were instantly dismissed.

While the restrictions and the enforcement were emphasized, the government also found room to provide incentives for the sale of liquor, with municipalities being offered half of the profits from its sale. Prohibitionists, not surprisingly, described the money as a bribe. Nevertheless, the government appeared to have taken a prudent middle course. The hated bar and public drinking were both banished, but imbibing unobtrusively in the privacy of one's home was now acceptable. The rationale seemed to be "out of sight — out of mind."

A powerful three-member Liquor Control Board (LCB), with extraordinary powers, was organized to administer the new government business. Only Cabinet could alter the Board's decisions, and not even the courts could review their findings. Naturally enough, patronage was carefully built into the system, as all employees of the LCB served at the will of the government in Victoria. At first, everything was done to make the "boozeoriums" as unfriendly as possible. The stores were dark, forbidding and heavily curtained, with only a small sign to indicate what was for sale. In each of the larger outlets, three white male clerks served the public. The first carefully examined a buyer's liquor permit, the second received the cash and placed a written order, and the third delivered the goods.

The government stores were an immediate success when they opened on June 15. Within a week, seventeen stores had opened, and by March 1922 there was at least one store in each of thirty-two of the province's thirty-nine electoral districts.[1] Three different full-strength brews miraculously appeared: Cascade Beer from BC Breweries, Silver Spring Beer from Victoria Brewery, and ale from a Fernie brewery. A dozen quarts of beer ran to two dollars, and the cost of a barrel was set at twenty dollars. Hard liquor was priced higher to encourage the use of beer rather than spirits; a bottle of good Scotch cost more than five dollars. Extra help had to be called into the Vancouver stores, and the clerks were "kept hard at it, with scarcely a breathing space until one o'clock when the rush began to abate." Tellingly, an estimated 75 percent were American customers escaping their own prohibition.[2]

After such a long dry stretch, many remained confused about how the new system worked. Some showed up at liquor stores trying to buy their five-dollar permits, not realizing that these could only be had at the motor licensing branches of the Provincial Police. Customers often demanded glasses, mugs, corkscrews or bottle openers from salesmen; or asked to be directed to the nearest vacant lot where their purchase could be easily and speedily disposed of. Some even politely inquired if they could not quietly consume their purchases in the store itself, which often had benches along the wall similar to those previously found in saloons.[3]

All near-beer jitney bars had been ordered closed, and a mock ceremony involving more than 1,500 Americans and British Columbians gathered at the border town of Huntington, Washington, to bid what was termed a fond farewell to "the obsequies of that arch-impostor, Near Beer alias Soapy Dopewater." It was commented that "legal troubles brought about his end, but he will be greatly missed in town, and people are already remarking how quiet everything has become since he departed." It was also ironically observed that human nature is fickle, and that "some are crying, 'le roi est mort, vive le roi,' while they prepare to give the true John Barleycorn a royal welcome."[4]

Veterans clubs, however, continued to sell near-beer (and presumably the stronger brew as well — but no spirits) in defiance of the government. They announced that they would continue to serve *bona fide* members, claiming that soldiers were bringing in their own legal refreshment, and that veterans clubs were merely serving it for a fee. These friendly clubs had a relaxed atmosphere, and were non-profit with a closed membership. They allowed patrons to "pool" their liquor, which effectively made booze available to all club members and their guests. Guards were posted at club entrances in Vancouver to admit only certified members, and the Provincial Police were barred unless they produced a search warrant. When the LCB refused to deliver to the clubs, the owners simply had their beer sent to another address and hauled it to the club themselves. Forty-six bars and hotels immediately applied to become "clubs," in many cases having nothing to do with servicemen. It seemed like a return to the good old days. In Vancouver, "club" beer sold for a reasonable twenty-five cents, with no trouble from the police — at first.

The decision by the clubs to bypass the law put Oliver's government in a difficult position. If the public drinking law was enforced in these clubs, the heroes of the Great War would be furious, and the results would be felt later at the ballot box. But if the government allowed the sale of near-beer to soldiers (which had been legal for toddlers just the day before), the government would be seen as weak and vacillating. Acute paralysis set in. When asked about the clubs, Attorney-General Farris claimed that no information concerning the violations of the law had been supplied to his department, and that there were "bigger fish to fry" in chasing illicit whiskey peddlers: "We are taking vigorous steps to stop the bootlegger." The real problems, he claimed, were to be found in bootlegging: "Unless the bootlegger is stopped we cannot secure proper enforcement of government control, or keep public administration on a high level."[5] Having refused to say that he would prosecute the clubs, it should have been no surprise to Farris when, a few days later, a story appeared on the front page of the *Vancouver Province* claiming that the Attorney-General had decided to allow beer to be served in the veterans clubs after all. Farris indignantly denied the story: "I will insist on the law being enforced," he trumpeted.

These words sparked a beer battle royal, with the government, frustrated prohibitionists and police pitted against veterans, hotel owners, and those wanting a return to public drinking. The government moved aggressively against the clubs, using municipal dry squads and their own liquor "secret service." The charters of dozens of clubs were summarily cancelled, and provincial constables were assigned to accompany beer deliveries to ensure that no shipments were sent to illegal destinations. Over the next year, hundreds were charged with selling beer, and the courts became thronged with onlookers hoping to catch a glimpse of secretive undercover Dry Squad operatives. Inspector Sutherland of the Vancouver Dry Squad did not mince words: "We are out to clean out every hotel bar and club where beer is being sold. While there has been somewhat of a lull during the past few days in carrying out raids, we have been busy securing evidence, and from now on expect to have a busy time of it."[6] He claimed to be sorry for the hoteliers who had recently opened their businesses, but maintained that no exceptions could be made. He was only enforcing the law.

In the first six months of 1922, a total of 679 cases of contraband were presented to the courts in Vancouver. Yet it was apparent that the provincial judges sympathized with the soldiers, when they ruled that a club was not a "person" under the Act, and thus could not be prosecuted. In another case, the judge declared that beer was not a "liquor," because a government seal had not been applied to every bottle. By 1923 the courts had accepted the argument that a club could not be charged with illegal sale, so long as the drinker provided his own drink and paid a token sum for service. In response, the government came up with the $100 LCB club licence, which allowed clubs to hold a patron's liquor for a small fee. Any establishment lacking such a licence was declared a public place where drink was prohibited. The first licences began to appear in 1924; not surprisingly, most went to veterans clubs.[7]

A major cause of the government's weakening resolve was money — lots of it. Every municipality received a generous portion of the net liquor revenues, based on population, with the rest going to a reserve fund in Victoria. When the first "dividend" checks arrived in December 1921, many were amazed. After only six months, Vancouver collected $110,000, Victoria $35,000, Nanaimo $ 8,000. The grand total for the province was a princely $200,000.[8] Money continued to pour in. In 1922 the government sold $15,200,000 worth of booze; and in 1923, $17 million worth. By 1923, liquor monies accounted for 15 percent of government income. Ironically, liquor, which had been considered the epitome of evil only three years before, was now saving the province from financial ruin.

At the same time as the profits from the sale of liquor were piling up, the opportunities for patronage, graft and corruption were multiplying. The new Liquor Control Board and Police Commission were easily manipulated and became a prime target of the Liberal political machine. The first three appointees — A. M. Johnson, J. H. Falconer and W.N. Winsby — were Liberal party hacks whose first job was to sort through some five thousand applications to select the 250 lucky workers needed in the warehouses and liquor stores. It soon became evident that the Liberals were as happy to bend the rules as the Conservatives and some prohibitionists had been. Large consignments of beer and spirits destined for delivery outside the province miraculously disappeared and reappeared in various warehouses. Confiscated liquor was often returned to the former owner, and charges dropped. Within months, two of the three-man LCB were in trouble for buying a five-year option to purchase a government liquor warehouse for $150,000

— just after it had been appraised by the government for only $58,000. Bowser accused the Liberals of forming an organized "ring" that controlled all LCB purchases. Even some Liberals, particularly from the interior of the province, began to wonder about the flagrant patronage and bootlegging going on under their administration. Farris was finally forced to resign in December 1921, and was replaced by Alex Manson, no friend of the liquor trade.

The stink of corruption was so strong that the new Attorney-General refused to accept the post unless he was allowed to conduct a thorough examination of the Liquor Control Board. Col. Ross Napier, Superintendent of Assessors, chaired the investigation, and came down hard on Board Member J. H. Falconer. He accused him of forging vendor orders, ignoring other members, and acting as a one-man board. Even then, the government refused to release the Napier report, and Falconer remained on the LCB until all three members were "retired" in October 1924. The new board consisted of one member, Hugh Davidson, owner of the Gregory Tire Company in Vancouver. This consolidation of power only increased the opportunity for graft.

The LCB was also dogged by questions about product purity. The president of the Vancouver Liberal Association, C.C. Delbridge, and Liberal campaign manager, H.J. McLatchey, were implicated in a scheme to provide cheap watered-down liquor to government stores. The Liquor Board itself was accused of adulterating its product with "synthetic compounds and unknown brands of vile filth heretofore unknown even to bootleggers."[9] The leader of the opposition, Billy Bowser, gleefully battered away at the Attorney-General and the Liberal "politico-brewery machine." Bootlegging returned with a vengeance, and the police often refused outright to prosecute. Notable exceptions were the "Dry Squads" in Vancouver and other large towns, which pursued liquor sellers with great diligence and energy. The small municipal police forces were responsible for the vast majority of law enforcement in the province, but they were poorly paid and easily seduced by bootlegger bribes. As was well known, many policemen were drinkers themselves, and the most common infraction among police forces throughout Canada during this period was for being intoxicated on the job.

It seemed that whatever liquor legislation was enacted during this period, British Columbians found ways to evade the law and to profit from it. One could brew and distil booze of all colours and tastes, then bootleg it, smuggle it, import it, adulterate it, or turn it into a medical prescription, and make a reasonable living. In fact, the illicit booze trade was a small entrepreneur's dream. Unlike the traditional mining, logging and fishing industries, where a small minority at the very top took the lion's share of the profits, the bootlegger kept a much larger portion of the cash take. As long as this intoxicant was restricted, and the price remained relatively high, alcohol's tremendous appeal assured a steady clientele. These activities broke the law, but they also provided clothes for the children, food for the table, medicine for Grandpa and steady employment for workers during hard times. Not every bootlegger or moonshiner was a "kingpin."

British Columbia faced a number of vexing problems in suppressing bootlegging and establishing the supremacy of the LCB. The federal government had refused to reimpose the 1918 ban on inter-provincial import and export of alcohol, allowing the provinces to vote on the matter themselves. Thus, it was still legal to order from out of province — and liquor obtained this way was both cheaper than from the LCB, and completely unregulated. A bottle of passable rye sent from Alberta cost only $3.50, and one did not need to present a British Columbia Liquor Permit to purchase. By March 1922, 360,000 gallons of imported beer and 600,000 gallons of "foreign" spirits had flooded the province.[10] Of course, the high cost of alcohol from the LCB also provided a strong incentive for bootlegging. The average weekly wage in Vancouver in 1921 was just over $30 a week, and the cost of a liquor permit, bottle of rye and case of beer, ran to $12.50 — over two days' wages. Since not many could afford this kind of pricing in the depressed economy of the early twenties, the cheaper black market prices were hard to resist.

Federal tax policies also encouraged bootlegging. Ottawa had tripled its customs and excise duties on liquor and levied a 5-percent tax after Quebec and British Columbia embraced government control in 1921. But liquor sold to customers outside Canada was exempt. Canadian export companies could order liquor, ostensibly for resale outside the country, and legally avoid paying the federal taxes the LCB had to pay. Not surprisingly, however, much of this cheap, "for export" liquor never left the province, or was smuggled back in for Canadian consumption. The *Province* reported:

> For some weeks customs officers have been scouring the inlets and islands of the Gulf in an endeavor to intercept launches which were suspected of bringing back from one of the large ships sailing between Vancouver, New Westminster and Victoria with clearance papers for Mexican or Central American points, liquor that is now flooding the local markets in successful competition with the genuine article on which the government has paid customs dues.[11]

With a little juggling of paperwork, bootleggers were able to undersell provincial liquor stores handily, and still turn a good profit. By 1922, it was estimated that the government sold just half of the alcohol consumed in the province.

Victoria's hands were tied. It had no control over inter-provincial or foreign trade, and it could not even clamp down on beer brewers because that was under the control of the federal government. LCB appointees had to maintain a precarious balancing act. If prices were set too high, bootleggers would move in and undercut them. If it asked too little, the Board would be seen as encouraging drinking.

The presence of huge stockpiles of alcohol destined for the United States further complicated the picture. America's prohibition had made smuggling liquor into the States from Canada a great temptation. By 1924 the trade had become highly organized, and many of today's well-known families in British Columbia and across Canada made their fortunes smuggling liquor to the United States. Dominion authorities were slow at first in clamping down on international rum-runners. A dozen or more large cargo vessels held station off the California, Oregon and Washington coasts just outside the American jurisdiction limit, waiting for customers. The most notorious of these was the sailing ship *Malahat*, 245-feet long, and displacing 1,500 tons. She could carry a mind-boggling 84,000 cases in her hold with an additional 16,000 on deck. Inevitably, some of the large quantity of booze being smuggled to the United States ended up on the streets of Vancouver and Victoria, when the vessels failed to make a rendezvous. What was not sold in the United States could easily be sold, tax-free, in Canada. Customs seized a number of vessels in remote coastal areas of the province, such as the *Impala* with 500 cases of Scotch whisky on board and no papers.

When the Americans complained about the wholesale smuggling, the W.L.M. King government in Ottawa established a Royal Commission on Customs and Excise to hold hearings in 1926–1927 to investigate the charges. The Lemieux-Brown Commission met from Halifax to Vancouver and uncovered all manner of nefarious activities. It turned out that many of the major smugglers had powerful political connections on both sides of the border. In November 1926, the notorious Henry Reifel was called on to testify. Reifel and his two sons, Harry and George, ran the so-called Vancouver liquor ring through the Joseph Kennedy Export House, BC Distillers and Vancouver Breweries. Flamboyant and cocky, Reifel freely admitted that one of his salesmen had regularly made payments to liquor store employees, and that he had made over $100,000 in political contributions to Liberal politicians in the province over the preceding eighteen months. Reifel seemed disappointed with his "investment," since he urged the Commission to make these "campaign funds" illegal, for, as he said, "You never get any return on the money."[12]

To reduce the hemorrhaging of cash, British Columbia imposed high taxes on liquor brought into the province, but the revenues proved difficult to collect. Victoria also raised the cost of export licenses from $3,000 to $10,000, which reduced the number of outlets and slowed the flow slightly. It was Attorney-General Manson who came up with a creative idea in 1923 for controlling beer bootleggers. Five breweries in the lower mainland and Vancouver Island were formed into a cartel called the Amalgamated Brewers Agency. The government guaranteed each brewery a slice of the business if they agreed to sell exclusively to the LCB. The small breweries of the interior did not join the arrangement, but agreed to keep their beer away from the coast. The bootlegging of beer was reduced and the new competitors were cut off from the closed market. The idea proved surprisingly durable and was copied by other provinces.[13]

Continued pressure from the United States and the revealing testimony of the Royal Commission on Customs and Excise eventually led to the 1928 Importation of Intoxicating Liquors Act. The provinces were given a free hand to regulate liquor entering their borders, which effectively closed the importation loophole. By the late twenties, bootleggers and rum-runners were forced to move their center of operations to Tahiti and Mexico.

The question of smuggling aside, the proliferation of beer clubs across the province made it increasingly difficult for the government to justify the sale of beer without the bar. The volatile question of public drinking was again about to take center stage. The age-old tradition of settling matters over a sociable glass of beer was remembered with fondness. Furtively drinking in seclusion, shut up in one's home, seemed to many a strange perversion of custom. But the prohibition movement still had some influence, and many Moderationists opposed a return to the bar, as did Premier Oliver. The issue proved so contentious in 1921 that Oliver held several voice votes in the legislature for a referendum on public beer drinking. His own party split, and was further weakened.

In 1923, Attorney-General Manson again tried to resolve the impasse on beer drinking in public, this time with a plebiscite set for June 1924 — the same day as the provincial election. But the wording on the ballot was dangerously vague: "Do you approve of the sale of beer by the glass in licenced premises — without a bar under government control and regulation?" No one knew whether the results would apply to the province as a whole, or to individual electoral districts. A Local Option bill had failed in the legislature, but this sounded a lot like the same thing.

The prohibitionists were horrified. The WCTU, the People's Prohibition Association (now known as the British Columbia Prohibition Association), the Methodist Conference, the Federation of Nurses and the Local Council of Women rallied fiercely to oppose beer sold by the glass. Private sale, they argued, would reintroduce the idea of profit in liquor sales, which led straight to saloon hell. They also held up the bootleggers and the scandals within the LCB as proof that government control was doomed to fail. Opposing them were the hotel industry, the breweries, the veterans, the Moderation League and Labour. Once again they claimed that beer was food and the true drink of moderation. They also frequently cited the $700,000 in wages paid in the brewing industry alone: "The passage of the 'beer by the glass' plebiscite will reduce the consumption of imported spirits in favor of light, wholesome, cheaper beer made by B.C. workers from materials produced on B.C. farms."[14] In addition, they trotted out the old chestnut, that "beer drinkers are not drunkards."

Apathy, however, again ruled on the issue. People were distracted by their own problems and put off by the ambivalent wording of the plebiscite. Labour and business were fighting major battles just to keep people employed. The veterans already had beer in their clubs, and the die-hard prohibitionists had relegated themselves to the fringe. It was generally assumed that the beer drinkers would prevail, and Oliver's government amended the Liquor Act to allow beer by the glass in municipalities that voted for it. When all the votes on the plebiscite were counted, the results were the worst that could be expected. The measure both won and lost at the same time. The anti-beer forces achieved a narrow victory in numbers — 73,853 to 72,214. But a majority of twenty-three of the province's forty electoral districts accepted beer by the glass. In Burnaby it was approved by one vote, and in Vancouver by seventy-eight; but in Victoria the plebiscite lost by 2,000. Rural areas like Lillooet, Fernie, Mackenzie, and the Cariboo region were particularly enthusiastic with 69 percent or more in favour of beer.[15] Manson's grand plan to defuse the beer crises had seriously backfired.

To add to the demoralizing beer vote, Oliver's government had made few gains in the provincial election. The Liberals now held half of the forty-eight seats in the legislature and were facing seventeen Conservatives, three members of the Provincial Party and three Labour MLAs. To form a majority, Oliver would be forced to turn to the Independents, who were in favour of beer by the glass. But the plebiscite results confused everybody, and both sides claimed victory. Wets and drys alike began to clamour for their electoral mandate to be carried out. Major R.J. Burde, the Independent member from Alberni, complained that elimination of the bar had actually encouraged alcohol use among the youth, and forced people in general to drink secretly in squalor:

> If I had a boy, I would ten thousand times have him living under the old bar system than prohibition or this remarkable law. Under the old system you never saw a small boy or girl drunk. Now, in every dance hall the boys carry a mickey on the hip, and the young flappers of 16 drink out of them.[16]

Burde demanded that the government "stand up and take the verdict of the plebiscite" — whatever that was.

As might be expected, Oliver's weak administration vacillated, and many agreed that the divisive beer question should be shelved for a year. The *Daily Province* on November 6, 1924, argued that the sides were fatally deadlocked, and, quoting Polonius, claimed that it was "as reasonably safe to say that beer will not be sold by the glass as it is to say that day follows night." Manson compared the situation to two trains pulling against each other on an imaginary track. One locomotive was labelled "government control" and the other "the breweries." But if the issue was to be shelved for a period, this did not mean that the newspapers did not continue their tirades against the criminal bootleggers. The *Daily Province* argued that, "since the bootlegger is a resourceful individual, and he is not hampered by any scruples of conscience or regard for the law," the liquor administration "should be equally resourceful, should be able to make instant decisions and have the power to carry these decisions to effect."[17]

But even as the newspapers were continuing their crusades against the bootleggers, there were still many drinkers who legally bought some of their booze from the LCB, and liquor dividends continued to mount — Vancouver alone was taking in $400,000 a month. There were now fifty-eight clubs in the province, 81,541 individual permits, 6,326 beer permits, 71 for ministers of the gospel, and 84 for doctors.[18] The LCB had turned into a vast money-making machine, with the help of thousands of American liquor tourists.

For their part the Provincial Police recognized the new mood. In particular they were well aware of the difficulties in obtaining liquor from the LCB in remote areas, and would conveniently turn a blind eye when the rules were stretched — in particular, for the onerous permit requirement. One constable recalled later that the police often looked the other way at moderate bootlegging:

> We were well aware of what was going on. But we didn't get any brownie points for laying charges, so most of us used our own discretion. Most people up island could not easily get to an LCB so them paying a couple of bucks for someone else to supply them with a bottle was not considered a big thing. However, if there was any disturbance or complaints, we stopped it fast.[19]

Then, in mid-December 1924, the legislature unexpectedly voted on the question. People were becoming exasperated by the debate that had been going on for almost a decade, and were anxious to put it behind them. Liquor had been for sale for over three years, the veterans still had their clubs, and the sky had not fallen in.

The final vote in the legislature was twenty-eight in favour of beer by the glass, with fifteen opposed — a solid majority. Only Manson and one other Liberal voted against beer by the glass. The Attorney-General blamed the industry for the vote: "I have come to the conclusion that beer by the glass is not an issue raised by the people, but by the breweries. The percentage of people wanting beer is small. The whole pot has been kept boiling by the breweries."[20] Premier Oliver tearfully voted yes, saying that he had never cast a more reluctant vote in his life. The anti-liquor forces had suffered yet another crushing defeat. Liquor licences for "standard hotels only" were soon granted, and the new establishments opened in March 1925. By 1926 there were more than sixty in Vancouver, with thirteen on a single two-block stretch of Cordova Street.

Liquor regulations in any society tend towards the bizarre and capricious. There are so many picayune areas that seem to plead for attention — where booze can be drunk, what it will be (beer and/or hard liquor), how strong a brew, or what kind of décor, entertainment, food and furniture will be tolerated on the premises, what hours will it be open, and so on. The provincial government moved to regulate all of these areas. The new sites for public drinking bore little resemblance to the saloons of old. All vestiges of the bar were vanquished other than the beer. Even the language was changed as words such as "saloon," "tavern" or "bar-room" were forbidden. "Beer parlour" became the new appellation.

Patrons were not permitted to stand up or move around with their drinks; they sat and were served at small tables. This rule was intended to reduce fights and discourage the costly practice of "treating" with repeated calls for "full rounds for the house." Only one kind of draft or bottled beer was offered at a time, and the brand name could not be advertised. Soft drinks, food and even cigarettes were banned so as to encourage the workingman to return home for dinner. (Some argued that this had the opposite effect.) There was no credit or cheque-cashing. Lighting was poor, the furniture uncomfortable, and the walls without pictures.

Many of the silly and quaint rules that govern the sale and use of intoxicating liquor today in British Columbia can be traced to the early 1920s, although of course the rules have been under revision in the last decade. At that time, and up until fairly recently, all entertainment — including singing, dancing, musical instruments and games — was forbidden. Hundreds would gather in joyless, barn-like hotels, tossing back buckets of ten-cent glasses of beer — bored stiff with nothing to do but drink. Ironically, with no food or entertainment, drunkenness was all these establishments had to offer. Cocktail lounges were not allowed at all until the early 1950s, when the laws were liberalized under W.A.C Bennett. To this day, police still retain the right to search one's person or vehicle without a warrant if they believe that one is keeping or distributing liquor illegally. If you are drunk in a public place they can detain you for up to twenty-four hours until you sober up.

In the years immediately after beer parlours were introduced, women were discouraged from visiting these new drinking factories for fear that their very presence would encourage immoral acts. It should be said, however, that while Quebec, Saskatchewan and Manitoba turned women away completely, British Columbia, with its permissive past, was somewhat more tolerant about allowing women to drink in public with the men. At first, the numbers were few, for in 1925 women earned just two-thirds of a man's wage and they still coped with many responsibilities at home in households dominated by "old fashioned" male relatives who preferred not to see their daughters and wives frequenting the bar. These patriarchal prejudices were widely held, and soon many communities began to exert pressure on hotels not to serve women at all. Once again it appeared that prohibitionists had found an emotive issue to excite the electorate. New Westminster and Revelstoke held local plebiscites, which upheld the ban on women. The Vancouver Anti-beer League raised $10,000 for yet another beer plebiscite, and it seemed for a while that there would be another vote on alcohol.

On the other hand, it had also become apparent that the fear of large numbers of women being corrupted by drunkenness was overblown. A weekend survey of Vancouver beer parlours in 1926 found only 284 women seated quietly among 2,396 men.[21] That same year, the Attorney-General's office advised the LCB and Hotel Association that they could not legally exclude woman, and a "gentlemen's agreement" was worked out, which did exactly that — exclude women. But the arrangement was voluntary, and when some hotel owners refused to comply, it fell apart. In 1927, a compromise was worked out in which there would be two separate rooms for drinkers — one for single men, and the other for women and their escorts. The areas would have separate entrances, so that there would be no opportunity for single men and women to meet and conspire to commit immoral acts together.

And so, true prohibition (for non-Natives) ended in British Columbia in March 1925. People looked back over the past decade as if it had been a dream. After the war, the sacrifices, the moral posturing, the never-ending plebiscites and referenda, and all the hard times, little had really changed. H.F. Gadsby, a Toronto journalist, wrote a fitting epitaph in *Maclean's* in 1919:

> Did somebody slip something over on us while the casualty lists blinded our eyes with tears? Did the cold water people get by while we were looking the other way? Was Prohibition a mood — all blue — or was it a conviction? Did we give up drink because giving up things was the fashion — horse races, baseball, banquets, time, money — all as nothing compared with the lives our boys gave up on the battle field? Did we give it up because it was the easiest way of martyrizing ourselves — or suffering something for the war which implied personal discomfort? Why did we give it up? And when we gave it up did we mean it?[22]

CONCLUSION

IN TODAY'S WORLD, the farce of drug prohibition repeats itself over and over with numbing regularity. It really does not seem to matter whether the intoxicant is dangerous or benign, whether it is addictive or only a social custom. Crystal meth, cocaine, heroin, marijuana, designer drugs, model airplane glue, tobacco, tea and coffee have all had their moments of prohibition, with the same results. In a pattern that has become all too familiar, artificial scarcity of a popular drug will inevitably lead to higher prices, a black market, and astonishing sums of illicit cash. Making something illegal does not remove it from the market. The sea of "black" dollars acts as an irresistible lure for the criminal element, and siphons away valuable tax revenues. In extreme cases, this money will lead to savage turf wars between dealers, and an epidemic of thefts as the poor struggle to pay for high-priced drugs. It also empowers crooked judges and politicians, encourages corruption and cronyism, leads to poisonous adulterated substitutes, generates contempt for the rule of law, and creates a parasitic bureaucracy dependent upon continued prohibition for its livelihood.

Yet drug prohibition has never worked. Indeed, it is impracticable even in the most tightly controlled environment. High security prisons are a notorious example: In spite of all the precautions, drugs always seem to find their way into the hands of the most isolated of inmates. To be sure, certain forms of substance control can create an appearance of successful prohibition, but closer examination shows this to be an illusion. For example, it is possible to prohibit the use of rare and unknown intoxicants. Khat, a plant stimulant popular in the Horn of Africa, has been banned in Canada for the last decade. There is no supply of the drug here, and most people have never even heard of it. Some have argued that khat prohibition has been a rousing success in Canada. But is this really prohibition? When one tries a similar ban in Ethiopia or Somalia, the use of this enormously popular and available drug does not decline. Following the usual pattern, the price goes up and it goes underground.

It is also true that the abolition of drugs and alcohol can be successful in small, tightly knit communities united under a strong ideology. These kinds of groups have routinely shunned practices they see as evil. William Duncan's Native community of Metlakatla in northern British Columbia is a good example. Drink there was never a problem, as members were united in their hatred of alcohol, and transgressors were immediately expelled. Joseph Smith's utopian Mormon settlements held similar views as did the ill-fated David Koresh community in Waco, Texas. Again, this is not really prohibition. These constraints were not written up as a law that everyone had to obey or go to jail. Rather they were self-imposed, based on moral and religious belief. Anyone could drop out of these communities. The lesson here is that the decision to abstain from any drug is a personal one, embraced voluntarily by the individual. When a ban is arbitrarily laid down by the state it becomes a burden rather than a means of self-empowerment.

Intellectual and religious diversity are the mortal enemies of prohibition. A large complex community with many differing viewpoints makes it impossible for people to agree on the social covenant necessary to make it work. And that is our present direction. We are becoming more diverse, more complicated and bigger in all respects. The chances of mounting a successful drug prohibition are receding even further as the years pass.

With such a record of dismal failure, why is this bankrupt solution proffered again and again to a gullible public? To be sure, there is a sincere desire to reduce the use of the drug, particularly if it is clearly harmful. Prohibition seems to offer a seductively simple solution to a very complex problem. It gives the appearance of concern and action while removing drug abusers from public sight. At first, people feel the situation is improving — the problem is shoved under the table and fades from view. But the seeming victory is a cruel illusion, doomed to failure. Moreover, as has been seen, prohibition can serve many masters. Paradoxically, lessening drug use often seems to be the last thing rulers are really concerned about. Prohibition's great appeal is that it allows central authorities unquestioned social control over individuals and groups. First Nations had their alcohol, Chinese their opium, Blacks their crack cocaine, beats and hippies their marijuana, and the ravers their ecstasy. In each of these cases, drug laws were specially drafted and used against these groups, which were perceived to be a physical or "cultural" threat to society. Similar laws are routinely used today all over the world to intimidate "trouble-makers" of all stripes, colours and religion.

An unfortunate side effect is that the drug enforcers themselves can become heavily addicted to prohibition. Power, once ceded, is not easily relinquished. Catching drug violators becomes a bureaucratic raison d'etre, as important as running down murderers and thieves. Even though users themselves are usually peaceful or debilitated, they often receive a disproportionate amount of attention and jail time. They are also easy prey. It seems likely that governments and police will continue strongly to resist any reduction in present drug laws because it cuts their budgets, reduces their power and makes them redundant.

On the positive side, the social control created by the 1917 prohibition worked to unite Canadian society against an enemy far more dangerous than booze — the German military juggernaut. It provided citizens with a sense of active participation during a dark and gloomy time. As the insane carnage continued, people felt helpless, for there was nothing they could do to alter the horrific events being played out in Europe. Making the personal sacrifice of abstaining from alcohol created the sense of *doing something* for the war effort — with the added advantage that anyone over twenty-one could freely participate. These personal sacrifices boosted sagging morale, and helped keep the home front focused on the monumental war effort.

An intriguing question lingers. What about gangster violence? For America, the spectacular failure of prohibition brought with it the rattle of automatic gunfire, the screech of tires racing down dark city streets, staggering riches in illicit cash, and solemn mourners at countless funerals. That did not happen in Canada. Nothing during our country's prohibition ever came close to this level of mayhem. James Gray noted that "in western Canada no one even punched anyone else in the nose" during prohibition, and that Canadians were much more likely to sue their enemies in court than take more drastic measures.

The answer lies partly in population dynamics. Canada had only one-tenth of the population of the United States, and the huge sums of money generated in America dwarfed the small change produced here. Even during the height of the rum-running craze, most of the profits from Canadian liquor flowed south. Once the boatloads of smuggled booze arrived in the United States, the shipments were quickly broken down into cases, bottles and drinks, increasing in value at each step of the process. Large criminal syndicates battled it out in cities like Chicago, squabbling for a piece of the liquor action. The street wars reached their peak in the early 1930s, and by the end of American prohibition in 1933, several thousand had died. While it is true that Canadians largely eschewed violence, they were not passive in their objections to prohibition. It is hard to imagine any other period in our history when normally law-abiding citizens became so defiant, willful and contemptuous of legal authority.

Some intoxicants can be a terrible evil. Addicts become enslaved, fall ill, and die in misery, a burden on society. No one wants to encourage such deadly habits. But using the law to forbid the use of intoxicants is worse. Prohibition unleashes corrupting forces that strike at the very heart and soul of society. The use and abuse of intoxicants is a complex matter that is inextricably bound to democratic freedoms and personal privacy. As this book has shown, governments should tread lightly in this area: heavy-handed attempts to ban the use of these substances will inevitably fail, bringing grief to both the government and the individual.

APPENDICES

APPENDIX TABLE NO. 1

THE PROHIBITION ERA IN CANADA

	YEAR PROVINCE WENT DRY	GOV'T CONTROL OF DRINKING	IN STORES IN PUBLIC DRINKING
Prince Edward Island	1901	1948	1964
Manitoba	1916	1923	1928
Nova Scotia	1916	1930	1948
Alberta	1916	1924	1924
Ontario	1916	1927	1934
Saskatchewan	1917	1925	1935
New Brunswick	1917	1927	1961
British Columbia	1917	1921	1925
Newfoundland	1917	1925	1925
Yukon	1918	1921	1925
Quebec	1919	1919	1921

(Heron, 270)

APPENDIX TABLE NO. 2

RATE OF CONVICTIONS FOR DRUNKENNESS	RATE OF CONVICTION UNDER LIQUOR CONTROL ACTS (PER 100,000 AGED FIFTEEN OR OLDER)
1913 — 2,599	232
1914 — 2,824	119
1915 — 1,779	73
1916 — 688	87
1917 — 696	169
1918 — 225	235
1919 — 284	169
1920 — 808	391
1921 — 643	372
1922 — 277	385
1923 — 359	298
1924 — 371	309
1925 — 427	393

RATE OF DEATH FOR ALCOHOLISM	RATE OF DEATH FROM LIVER CIRRHOSIS (PER 100,000 AGED TWENTY OR OVER)
1913 — 16.5	7.6
1914 — 10.6	6.6
1915 — 5.9	6.3
1916 — 5.9	4.9
1917 — 5.8	4.9
1918 —	—
1919 — 3.1	2.8
1920 — 2.7	4.9
1921 — 3.3	3.6
1922 — 4.3	5.1
1923 — 3.9	5.3
1924 — 7.3	6.7
1925 — 5.5	7.0
1926 — 5.8	4.5
1927 — 5.4	6.5
1928 — 6.4	6.6
1929 — 9.4	7.8

(Popham and Schmidt, 69–70 & 108–109)

NOTES

CHAPTER 1

1 Ronald K. Siegel, *Intoxication: Life in Pursuit of the Artificial Paradise* (New York: E.P. Dutton, 1989), 10.

2 Edward Behr, *Prohibition: Thirteen Years That Changed America* (New York: Arcade Publishing, 1996), 23.

3 Norman, H. Clark, *Deliver Us From Evil: An Interpretation of American Prohibition* (New York: W.W. Norton and Company, 1976), 8.

4 Behr, 10.

5 Behr, 16.

6 Adele Perry, *On the Edge of Empire: Gender, Race, and the Making of British Columbia, 1849–1871* (Toronto: University of Toronto Press, 2001), 92.

7 John Kobler, *Ardent Spirits: The Rise and Fall of Prohibition* (New York: First Da Capo Press, 1993), 172.

8 Dashaway Association of Victoria, *Constitution and By-Laws* (Victoria: Amor de Cosmos, 1860), 8.

9 *Royal Commission on the Liquor Traffic,* reprint of the 1896 edition (Toronto: Coles Publishing Company, 1973), 21.

10 Lynne Bowen, *Three Dollar Dreams* (Lantzville, BC: Oolichan Books, 1987), 248.

11 Richard L. Sweet, *The Directory of Canadian Breweries (Past and Present)*, 2nd Edition (Saskatoon, Sask: Self Published, 1996), 20–35.

12 Sweet, 20–35.

13 *Cariboo Sentinel* in *The Illustrated History of British Columbia* by Terry Reksten (Vancouver: Douglas & McIntyre, 2001), 74.

14 Albert John Hiebert, "Prohibition in British Columbia," MA Thesis in History, Simon Fraser University (1969), 14–15.

15 Emily Carr, *The Book of Small* (New York: Oxford University Press, 1943), 85.

16 Lynne Bowen, *Boss Whistle: The Coal Miners of Vancouver Island Remember* (Lantzville, BC: Oolichan Books, 1982), 217.

CHAPTER 2

1 *Nanaimo Gazette,* 28 August, 1865: 1

2 José Mariano Moziño, *Noticias de Nutka: An Account of Nootka Sound, 1792,* translated by H. Wilson Engstrand (Vancouver: Douglas & McIntyre, 1970), 21.

3 James G. Swan, *The Northwest Coast: Or, Three Year's Residence in Washington Territory* (Seattle: University of Washington Press, 1992), 155–56.

4 Edwin M. Lemert, *Alcohol and the Northwest Indians* (Los Angeles: University of California Press, 1954), 351.

5 *Nanaimo Gazette,* 2 October 1865: 3.

6 *Nanaimo Gazette,* 18 September 1865: 3.

7 *Nanaimo Gazette,* 28 August 1865: 1.

8 W. Kaye Lamb, "The Diary of Robert Melrose, Part 2," *British Columbia Historical Quarterly,* 8 (July 1943): 199.

9 Barry M. Gough, *Gunboat Frontier: British Maritime Authority and West Coast Indians, 1846–1890* (Vancouver: University of British Columbia Press, 1984), 91.

10 Nicholas J.S. Simons, "Liquor Control and the Native Peoples of Western Canada," MA Thesis, Simon Fraser University (1992), 94.

11 *Nanaimo Gazette,* 28 August 1865: 1.

12 Gough, 220–23.

13 *Victoria Daily Press,* 27 May 1862: 3.

14 *British Colonist*, 13 November 1865: 3.

15 Roland L. De Lorme, "Liquor Smuggling in Alaska 1867–1899," *Pacific Northwest Quarterly*, 66 (1975): 145–52.

16 Gough, 91.

17 *British Colonist*, 5 January 1866: 3.

18 *British Colonist*, 29 December 1865: 3.

19 *Nanaimo Gazette*, 5 February 1866: 1.

20 Robert A. Campbell, *Sit Down and Drink Your Beer: Regulating Vancouver's Beer Parlours 1925–1954* (Toronto: University of Toronto Press, 2001), 96–97.

21 Renisa Mawani, "In Between and Out of Place: Racial Hybridity, Liquor and the Law in Late 19th and Early 20th Century British Columbia," *Canadian Journal of Law and Society*, 15 (2000): 12–16.

22 Robert A. Campbell, "'A Fantastic Rigmarole': Deregulating Aboriginal Drinking in British Columbia 1945–62," *BC Studies*, 141 (Spring 2004): 83.

23 Megan Schlase, "Liquor and the Indian Post WWII," *BC Historical News*, 29 (Spring 1996): 27.

24 Schlase, 26.

25 Campbell, *Sit Down*, 97–98.

26 Lemert, 308–309.

27 Campbell, *Fantastic Rigmarole*, 89–91.

28 *Vancouver Sun*, 15 December 1951: 43.

29 *Victoria Daily Times*, 14 December 1951: 30.

30 *Vancouver Sun*, 15 December 1951: 4.

31 *Victoria Daily Times*, 13 December 1951: 1.

32 *Vancouver Sun*, 15 December 1951: 43.

33 *Daily Colonist*, 16 December 1951: 51

34 Campbell, *Sit Down*, 100.

35 Campbell, *Fantastic Rigmarole*, 95.

36 Campbell, *Fantastic Rigmarole*, 98–99.

37 *Vancouver Daily Times*, 3 July 1962: 2.

38 Campbell, *Fantastic Rigmarole*, 100.

39 Schlase, 28–29.

40 Schlase, 29.

41 Lemert, 336.

42 Campbell, *Sit Down*, 103

43 Gough, 241.

CHAPTER 3

1 R. Douglas Francis, Richard Jones, and Donald B. Smith ed. *Canadian History Since Confederation*, 2nd ed. (Toronto: Holt Rinehart, and Winston of Canada Ltd, 1992), 222.

2 Richard Allen, "The Social Gospel as the Religion of Agrarian Revolt" in *The West and the Nation*, edited by Carl Berger and Ramsay Cook (Toronto: McClelland and Stewart, 1976), 178.

3 Craig Heron, *Booze: A Distilled History* (Toronto: Between the Lines, 2003), 141.

4 Daniel Francis ed., *The Encylopedia of British Columbia* (Madeira Park BC: Harbour Publishing, 2000), 17, 572.

5 Hiebert, Thesis, 24.

6 Betty Keller, *On the Shady Side: Vancouver 1886–1914* (Ganges BC: Horsdal and Schubart, 1986), 33–34, 70.

7 *Daily Colonist*, 14 June 1883.

8 Hiebert, Thesis, 88.

9 Harold Tuttle Allen, *Forty Years' Journey: The Temperance Movement in British Columbia to 1900* (Victoria: self published, 1981), 52.

10 Harold T. Allen, 57.

11 Hiebert, Thesis, 12.

12 Lynne Stonier-Newman, *Policing a Pioneer Province: The BC Provincial Police 1858–1950* (Madeira Park, BC: Harbour Publishing, 1991), 51–52.

13 Stonier-Newman, 44.

14 Heron, 170.

15 Hiebert, Thesis, 51.

16 Hiebert, Thesis, 54–60.

17 Hiebert, Thesis, 60.

18 Martin Robin, *Rush for Spoils: The Company Province, 1871–1933* (Toronto: McClelland and Stewart, 1972), 128.

CHAPTER 4

1 Robin, 116, 139.

2 Robin, 146.

3 Reksten, 181.

4 *Daily Colonist*, 5 January 1919: 10–11.

5 *Daily Colonist*, 2 August 1917: 1.

6 Canada Food Board Pamphlet, *Food Conservation Policy to be Observed in the Homes of the Province of British Columbia, BC* Committee (1918), 4.

7 Hiebert, Thesis, 67.

8 *World,* 26 August 1915.

9 People's Prohibition Association Minutes, 2 December 1915, in British Columbia Alcohol Research and Education Council, 1915–1972, Victoria: BC Archives, MS-0017, box 29.

10 Robin, 132.

11 PPA Minutes, 14 April 1917.

12 PPA Minutes, 27 July 1916.

13 *Prohibition Act? The Truth about the Prohibition Act* (Merchants Protective Association, 1916).

14 "British Columbia Provincial Secretary Correspondence, 1913–1916," March 8, 1916.

15 Robert A. Campbell, *Demon Rum or Easy Money: Government Control of Liquor in British Columbia from Prohibition to Privatization* (Ottawa: Carleton University Press, 1919), 30.

16 *BC Federationist,* 14 January 1916: 2.

17 *Daily Colonist,* 17 August 1917.

18 *BC Fderationist,* 8 October 1915: 1.

19 W.D. Bayley, *Labour and Liquor: An Appeal to the Intelligence and Legitimate Self-Interest of the Workers of BC* (Peoples Prohibition Movement Pamphlet, 1915).

CHAPTER 5

1 *Daily Colonist,* 19 August 1917: 7.

2 *Nanaimo Free Press,* 13 September 1916: 2.

3 *Prohibition Act?,* 22.

4 *The Real Truth About the Prohibition Act,* People's Prohibition Movement Pamphlet (1916), 8.

5 *Shall We Compensate the Liquor Man?,* People's Prohibition Movement Pamphlet (Vancouver, 1915), 4.

6 Margaret Alice Beckwith, Papers and Scrapbook (1915).

7 *Daily Colonist,* 9 September 1916: 12.

8 *World,* 19 August 1916: 14.

9 *British Columbian,* 13 September 1916: 8.

10 Campbell, *Demon Rum,* 20.

11 Mimi Ajzenstadt, "The Medical-Moral Economy of Regulation: Alcohol Legislation in B.C. 1871–1925," PHD dissertation, Simon Fraser University (1992), 162–64.

12 Robert Craig Grown and Ramsay Cook. *Canada 1896–1921: A Nation Transformed* (Toronto: McClelland and Stewart Ltd, 1974), 24.

13 *British Columbian,* 2 September 1916: 4.

14 Alfred Lewis ed., *Facts and Figures Against Prohibition: How to Vote* (Burnaby: Burnaby Printing and Publishing Company, 1915), 8, 15.

15 *Nanaimo Free Press,* 8 September 1916: 2.

16 *World,* 9 August 1916: 1.

17 *World,* 11 August 1916: 8.

18 *BC Federationist,* 18 August 1916: 1.

19 *BC Federationist,* 18 August 1916: 1–2.

20 *Workers Manual Prohibition Campaign (Private and Confidential for Prohibition Workers Only),* People's Prohibition Movement Pamphlet (1916), 5–7.

21 Tim Cook, "'More Medicine Than a Beverage': Demon Rum and the Canadian Trench Soldier of the First World War," *Canadian Military History,* 9, no. 1 (Winter 2000) 7.

22 Paul Fussell, *The Great War and Modern Memory* (New York: Oxford University Press, 1975) 46.

23 Jane Dewar, *True Canadian War Stories from Legion Magazine* (Ontario: Prospero Books, 1989), 6.

24 Cook , 17.

25 Cook, 10.

CHAPTER 6

1 PPA Minutes, 4 and 12 July, 1916.

2 *Daily Colonist,* 31 March 1917: 5.

3 *Statutes of British Columbia,* Chapter 50, 238.

4 "Commission on the Overseas Vote in Connection with the British Columbia Prohibition Act" (Victoria: June/July 1917), Day 1, 4.

5 "Commission," Day 1, 6.

6 "Commission," Day 8, 1–7.

7 "Commission," Day 2, 17.

8 "Commission," Day 3, 62.

9 "Commission," Day 5, 20.

10 "Commission," Day 1, 24.
11 "Commission," Day 5, 13.
12 "Commission," Day 5, 48–49.
13 "Commission," Day 3, 57–60.
14 *Daily Colonist,* 14 August 1917: 4.
15 *Daily Colonist,* 15 August 1917: 8, 12.
16 *Daily Colonist,* 16 August 1917: 7.
17 Hiebert, Thesis, 109.
18 *Daily Colonist,* 13 March 1920: 1.
19 *Daily Colonist,* 13 March 1920: 16.

CHAPTER 7

1 Stonier-Newman, 56, 84, 94, 118, 144.
2 Stonier-Newman, 69.
3 Stonier-Newman, 113.
4 Stonier-Newman, 115–16.
5 Prohibition Files, 1917–1925, in "British Columbia Provincial Police Force, Superintendent," letter dated November 1917.
6 Prohibition Files, Box 1, File 1, letter dated November 1917.
7 Prohibition Files, Box 1, File 1, letter dated 7 May 1920.
8 Prohibition Files, Box 1, File 2, letter dated 19 March 1920.
9 Prohibition Files, Box 1, File 2, letter dated 15 May 1920.
10 Prohibition Files, Box 1, File 4, letter dated 23 January 1918.
11 Prohibition Files, Box 1, File 4, letter dated 22 May 1919.
12 Prohibition Files, Box 1, File 4, letter dated 22 February 1919.
13 Prohibition Files, Box 1, File 2, letter dated 22 April 1920.
14 Prohibition Files, Box 1, File 4, letter dated 8 July 1919.
15 Prohibition Files, Box1, File 4, letter dated 11 December 1919.
16 Bowen, *Boss Whistle,* 67.
17 Stonier-Newman, 119.
18 Prohibition Files, Box 4, File 23.
19 Prohibition Files, Box 2, File 2, report dated 25 June 1920.
20 Prohibition Files, Box 3, File 4, transcript dated 3 February 1920.
21 Stonier-Newman, 117.
22 *Daily Colonist,* 10 August 1950: 4.

CHAPTER 8

1 Hiebert, Thesis, 101–102
2 PPA Minutes, 30 March 1920.
3 *First Report by the Prohibition Commissioner on the BC Prohibition Act* (Victoria: 1920), 10.
4 Hiebert, Thesis, 111.
5 *Second Report by the Prohibition Commissioner on the BC Prohibition Act* (Victoria: 1921), Y5.
6 *First Report*, 7.
7 *Second Report*, Y9.
8 *First Report*, 7.
9 *First Report*, 5.
10 Bowen, *Boss Whistle*, 212.
11 *Daily Colonist*, 8 September 1920: 4.
12 *World*, 29 March 1920: 2.
13 Allen Winn Sneath, *Brewed in Canada: The Untold Story of Canada's 350-Year Old Brewing Industry* (Toronto: Dundurn Press, 2001), 116.
14 *Daily Colonist*, 12 December 1918: 7.
15 *Daily Colonist*, 12 December 1918: 11.
16 PPA Minutes, 27 August 1917.
17 *Daily Colonist*, 17 December 1918: 3.
18 PPA Minutes, 17 December 1918.
19 *Daily Colonist*, 17 December 1918: 3.
20 *Daily Colonist*, 15 December, 1918: 3.
21 *Daily Colonist*, 19 December 1918: 5.
22 *Daily Colonist*, 28 December 1918: 2.
23 *Daily Colonist*, 28 December 1918: 2.
24 *Daily Colonist*, 18 March 1919: 7.
25 J. Castell Hopkins, *The Canadian Annual Review of Public Affairs* (Toronto: The Annual Review Publishing Company, 1919), 796.
26 *Victoria Daily News*, 23 May 1919: 4.
27 *Daily Colonist*, 1 February 1919: 12.
28 "British Columbia Alcohol Research and Education Council, 1915–1972," letter dated March 30, 1920, Victoria: BC Archives, MS-0017, Box 14.
29 *Second Report*, Y6.
30 Hiebert, Thesis, 113.

31 *Victoria Daily Times*, 10 May 1919: 2.
32 *Victoria Daily Times*, 29 May 1919: 3–4.
33 "British Columbia Provincial Secretary Correspondence, 1913–1916," letter dated 7 November, 1919.
34 Robin, 177.

CHAPTER 9

1 *Daily Colonist*, 23 January 1918: 5.
2 James Morton, *Honest John Oliver* (London, England: J.M. Dent and Sons Ltd, 1933), 199.
3 Campbell, *Demon Rum*, 27.
4 *Daily Colonist*, 6 February 1919: 4.
5 *World*, 6 March 1919: 4.
6 *World*, 11 October 1920: 3.
7 MS-0017, Box 14, letter dated 8 February 1918.
8 MS-0017, Box 14, letter dated 21 March 1919.
9 Hiebert, Thesis, 119.
10 MS-0017, Box 14, letter dated 16 August 1919.
11 *World*, 9 February 1920: 1, 3.
12 Campbell, *Demon Rum*, 31.
13 *Daily Colonist*, letter to the editor, 11 September 1920: 15.
14 *Daily Colonist*, 19 October 1920: 4.
15 Hiebert, Thesis, 127.
16 Campbell, *Demon Rum*, 30.
17 Campbell, *Demon Rum*, 30–31.
18 Hiebert, Thesis, 129.
19 *World*, 21 October 1920: 1.
20 *World*, 21 October 1920: 1.
21 *Vancouver Daily Sun*, 21 October 1920: 3.
22 *World*, 21 October 1920: 3.

CHAPTER 10

1 Campbell, *Demon Rum*, 43.
2 *World*, 15 June 1921: 1; 16 June 1921: 1.
3 *World*, 17 June 1921: 1.
4 *World*, 15 June 1921: 1.

5 *World,* 18 June 1921: 2.
6 *World,* 13 December 1921: 1.
7 Campbell, *Demon Rum,* 49.
8 *World,* 20 December, 1921: 1.
9 Robin, 188.
10 Campbell, *Demon Rum,* 45.
11 *Daily Province,* 16 December 1924: 22.
12 Robert A. Campbell, "Liquor and Liberals: Patronage and Government Control in British Columbia, 1920–1928," *BC Studies,* 77 (Spring 1988): 48.
13 Campbell, *Liquor and Liberals,* 47.
14 *Daily Province,* 18 June 1924: 14.
15 Campbell, *Demon Rum,* 53.
16 *Daily Province,* 17 December 1924: 2.
17 *Daily Province,* 12 December 1924: 6.
18 *Daily Province,* 3 November 1924: 1.
19 Stonier-Newman, 158.
20 *Daily Province,* 17 December 1924: 2.
21 Heron, 290.
22 *Maclean's Magazine,* April 1919, in Gerald A. Hallowell, *Prohibition in Ontario, 1919–1923* (Toronto: Ontario Historical Society, 1972), 29–30.

BIBLIOGRAPHY

Ajzenstadt, Mimi. "The Medical-Moral Economy of Regulations: Alcohol Legislation in B.C., 1871–1925," PhD Dissertation. Simon Fraser University, 1992.

Allen, Harold Tuttle. *Forty Years' Journey: The Temperance Movement in British Columbia to 1900.* Victoria: privately published, 1981.

Allen, Richard. "The Social Gospel as the Religion of Agrarian Revolt," in *The West and the Nation,* edited by Carl Berger & Ramsay Cook. Toronto: McClelland and Stewart, 1976.

Barman, Jean. *The West Beyond the West.* Toronto: University of Toronto Press, 1991.

Barr, Andrew. *Drink: A Social History of America.* New York: Carroll and Graf, 1999.

Bartlett, Eleanor A. "Real Wages and the Standard of Living in Vancouver 1901–1929." *BC Studies,* 51 (Autumn 1981): 3–63.

Bayley, W.D.: *Labour and Liquor: An Appeal to the Intelligence and Legitimate Self-Interest of the Workers of BC.* People's Prohibition Movement pamphlet, 1915. SFU Library, CIHM #9-90050.

Beckwith, Margaret Alice. *Papers and Prohibition Scrapbook*, 1915. BC Archives.

Behr, Edward. *Prohibition: Thirteen Years That Changed America*. New York: Arcade Publishing, 1996.

Bowen, Lynne. *Boss Whistle: The Coal Miners of Vancouver Island Remember.* Lantzville, BC: Oolichan Books, 1982.

Bowen, Lynne. *Three Dollar Dreams*. Lantzville, BC: Oolichan Books, 1987.

"British Columbia Alcohol Research and Education Council, 1915–1972." Victoria: BC Archives, MS-0017.

"British Columbia Premiers Correspondence 1883–1933." Victoria: BC Archives, GR-0441, Boxes 95–133, 168–213.

"British Columbia Provincial Police Force, Superintendent, Prohibition Files, 1917–1925." Victoria: BC Archives, GR-1425, Boxes 1–4.

"British Columbia Provincial Secretary Correspondence, 1913–1916." Victoria: BC Archives, GR-0157, Box 2.

"British Columbia Provincial Secretary Correspondence, 1914–1918." Victoria: BC Archives, GR-0527, Box 4, and 5.

Brown, Robert Craig & Ramsay Cook. *Canada 1896–1921: A Nation Transformed*. Toronto: McClelland and Stewart Ltd., 1974.

Campbell, Robert A. *Demon Rum or Easy Money: Government Control of Liquor in British Columbia from Prohibition to Privatization*. Ottawa: Carleton University Press, 1991.

———. "'A Fantastic Rigmarole': Deregulating Aboriginal Drinking in British Columbia 1945–62." *BC Studies*, 141 (Spring 2004): 81–104.

———. "Ladies and Escorts: Gender Segregation and Public Policy in British Columbia Beer Parlours, 1925–1945." *BC Studies*, 105/106 (Spring/Summer 1995): 119–38.

———. "Liquor and Liberals: Patronage and Government Control in British Columbia 1920–1928." *BC Studies*, 77 (Spring 1988): 30–53.

———. *Sit Down and Drink Your Beer: Regulating Vancouver's Beer Parlours 1925–1954*. Toronto: University of Toronto University Press, 2001.

Canada Food Board, BC Committee. *Food Conservation Policy to be Observed in the Homes of the Province of British Columbia*, pamphlet, August, 1918. BC Archives.

Carr, Emily. *The Book of Small*. New York: Oxford University Press, 1943.

Clark, Cecil. *Tales of the British Columbia Provincial Police*. Sidney, BC: Gray's Publishing Ltd., 1971.

Clark, Norman H. *Deliver Us from Evil: An Interpretation of American Prohibition*. New York: W.W. Norton and Company, 1976.